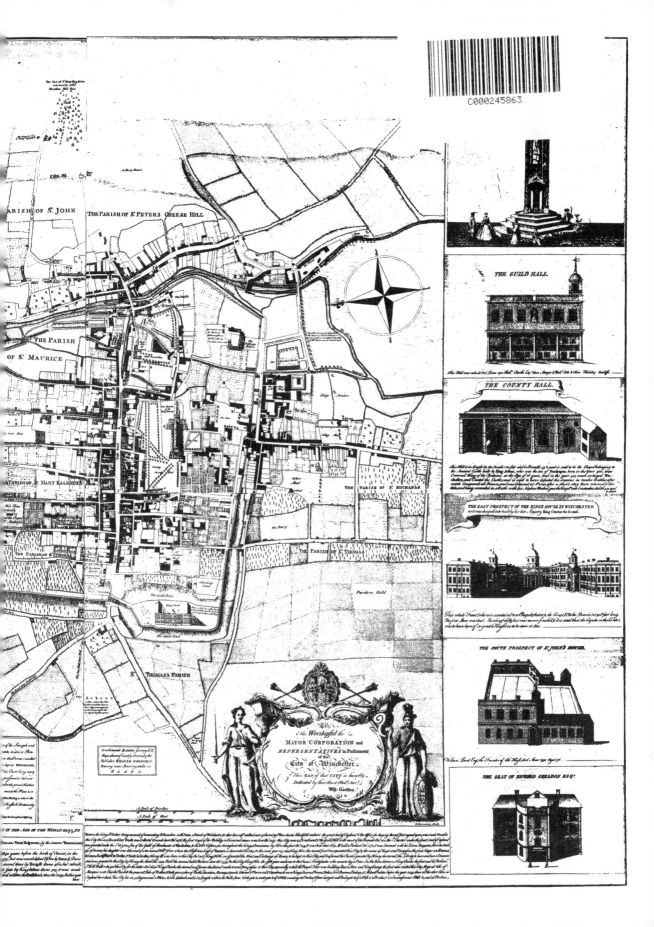

THE GUILD HALL.

THE COUNTY HALL.

THE EAST PROSPECT OF THE KING'S HOUSE IN WINCHESTER
as it was designed to be built by his late Majesty King Charles on the Ground.

THE SOUTH PROSPECT OF S.t JOHN'S HOUSE.

THE SEAT OF EDWARD SHELDON ESQ.r

To the Worshipful the
MAYOR CORPORATION and
REPRESENTATIVES in Parliament
of the
City of Winchester
This MAP of that CITY is humbly
Dedicated by their most Obed.t Serv.t
Will: Godson

WINCHESTER
A Pictorial History

To Andrew, Xmas 1995
with love
mother + father

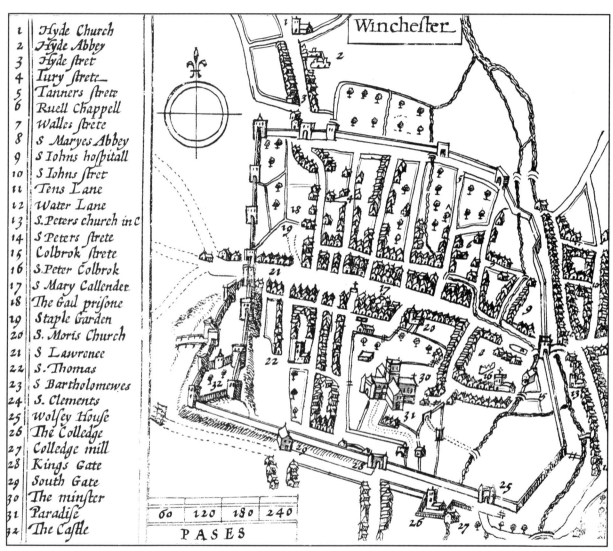

1	Hyde Church
2	Hyde Abbey
3	Hyde stret
4	Iury strete
5	Tanners strew
6	Ruell Chappell
7	Walles strete
8	S Maryes Abbey
9	S Iohns hospitall
10	S Iohns stret
11	Tens Lane
12	Water Lane
13	S Peters church in c
14	S Peters strete
15	Colbrok strete
16	S Peter Colbrok
17	S Mary Callender
18	The Gail prisone
19	Staple Garden
20	S. Moris Church
21	S Lawrence
22	S Thomas
23	S Bartholomewes
24	S Clements
25	Wolsey House
26	The Colledge
27	Colledge mill
28	Kings Gate
29	South Gate
30	The minster
31	Paradise
32	The Castle

Winchester

60 120 180 240

PASES

Winchester's street plan, *c*.1611, from an inset in John Speed's map of Hampshire (HRO 139M89, vol. 1, p.3). *(See* front and back end papers for maps of the city in 1750 and in 1805.)

WINCHESTER
A Pictorial History

Tom Beaumont James

Phillimore

1993

Published by
Phillimore and Co. Ltd.,
Shopwyke Manor Barn, Chichester, West Sussex

ISBN 0 85033 808 5

Printed and bound in Great Britain by
BIDDLES LTD.
Guildford, Surrey

I dedicate this book to my sons Edward and Richard, natives of Winchester (1985 and 1988), who give me enormous pleasure — even when interrupting progress on this book.

List of Illustrations

Frontispiece: Winchester's street plan, *c.*1611

Illustration Acknowledgements

The Author, 11, 43, 47, 81, 137, 141, 160; Kate Brooker, 73; John Crook, 1, 2, 3, 6, 8, 10, 12, 14, 16, 18, 20, 22, 24, 26, 28, 30, 32, 34, 36, 44, 78, 88, 91, 136, 149, 154, 159, 182, 194; John Crook/Dean and Chapter, 142, 147, 149, 182; John Crook/Hampshire County Library, 82; Hampshire County Library/Derek Dine, 42 (327/5/1), 57 (438/4/5), 59 (196/5/5), 65 (344/1/3), 67-8 (150/6/5), 84 (330/6/6), 85 (524/3/2), 92 (279/6/3), 94 (444/2/4), 95 (444/3/2), 96 (188/5/5), 107 (326/7/3), 108 (357/2/3), 109 (357/1/4), 110 (335/2/3), 116 (349/6/1), 119 (463/1/5), 129 (151/2/1), 130 (579/2/11), 134 (368/4/3), 153 (187/6/4), 171 (335/3/4), 173 (335/6/4), 177 (594/3/5), 185 (335/1/5), 189, (459/5/4), 190 (460/5/1), 191 (445/1/1); Fire Station Archive, 53; Friends of King Alfred's Motor Services, 72, 75, 77; David Fry: 157 (Airco); 29, 31, 39, 40, 54, 56, 58, 67, 70, 71, 74, 86, 89, 90, 93, 100, 102, 103, 105, 111, 113, 114, 115, 117, 118, 124, 128, 131, 133, 139, 143, 144, 145, 148, 150, 157, 164, 170, 172, 176, 178, 179, 180, 181, 186 (Beloe); 163, 165, 167 (Holliday); 158 (Kingsway); 114 (Rider); 27, 115, 102 (Wright); *Hampshire Chronicle*: 76; Hampshire Record Office: 9, (85M88/13), 15 (56M71/16/11081), 35 (65M89/Z250 (part)), 36 (56M71/1056), 37, (154M84W/6k), 38 (154M84W/6p), 48 (154M86W/10c), 49 (138M84W/15f), 51 (85M88/13), 60, 61 (85/M88/13 fos. 48, 47), 60, 63 (56M71/16/1106), 66 (154M84W/6h), 97 (56M71/13/856), 98 (85M88/13), 99 (85M88/13), 104, (56M71/15/1101), 152 (56M71/994), 159 (56M71/16/1087), 188 (56M71/15/1024); Tony Lee: 45, 46; Edward Roberts: 27, 41, 55, 69, 106, 120, 126, 127, 132, 144, 146, 158, 162, 166, 168, 169, 183, 184, 187; By Courtesy of the Trustees of the Victoria and Albert Museum: 87 (E222 1955); Winchester Museum Service: 4 (3599), 5 (7489), 7 (301), 13 (3565), 17 (3606A), 19 (3736), 21 (7380), 23 (10210), 25 (23796), 33 (7352), 50 (9985), 52 (4423), 55 (11016), 62 (10147), 64 (3758), 79 (3551), 80 (3626), 83 (3717), 101 (2642), 112 (2738+), 121 (3735), 122 (23786), 123 (23787), 125 (10673), 135 (5056), 138 (4440), 140 (3508), 146 (10979), 151 (3516), 155 (6934), 156 (3625), 161 (2084), 174 (13723), 175 (5094), 192 (5144), 193 (5219).

Foreword and Acknowledgements

Several books of photographs of Winchester already exist, notably *In and around Winchester*, by Edward Roberts (Oxley, 1977) and *Winchester: Seen and Remembered* by Philippa Stevens and Derek Dine (H.C.C., 1978). The former concentrated on the city and environs in the classic period of pictorial recording between about 1890 and 1930. In the latter Philippa Stevens selected 'historic' views of the city that are both familiar and unfamiliar, which Derek Dine then photographed. My book records a number of changes in the city in recent years and pictures that have not been made available before. However, no self-denying ordinance has been imposed to exclude views of topics used in previous books — that would have made for a very odd book indeed! Nor is this the last of its kind: Winchester City Museum, to take but one example, has over 20,000 pictures from which to choose, and in addition many thousands of further photographs in major collections not yet easily accessible to the browser. Winchester College, the Cathedral Library, the Hampshire Record Office, the Local Studies Library, the Heritage Centre and St Peter's Church all have further valuable collections to list but a few. Amongst the private collections known to the author, David Fry and Edward Roberts have some splendid examples and have been most generous in making them available to me. Every effort has been made to trace copyright holders and to obtain appropriate permissions, and it is hoped that even in a work of nearly 200 pictures there have been no omissions in this respect.

Many people have given most freely of their expertise and I thank them all most heartily. Kate Brooker hunted out her unique picture of the bypass; Derek Dine helped greatly from his collection; David Fletcher at the Tank Museum at Bovington explained the pictures of armoured vehicles when Michael Halsted put us in touch; David Fry's generosity in allowing me free rein within this collection provided a solid base; at the Hampshire Record Office, Pearl Andrews, Sarah Lewin and Gill Rushton were most prompt and helpful as were Graham Scobie at the archaeology unit and Ken Jones at Winchester fire station; Tony Lee once more provided his pictures; Karen Parker at the City Museum is a mine of information and has an unrivalled knowledge of the huge collections within her charge; Edward Roberts has checked drafts and given great support, practical advice, help and encouragement; Philippa Stevens and Maureen Gale and the staff of the Hampshire County Library, Local Studies Branch did everything possible to facilitate this work; Ian Shawyer of the Friends of King Alfred's Motor Services, and Chris Webb provided much information and a selection of photographs at very short notice; Tony Hunter at the Heritage Centre kindly offered help and enabled the solving of problems. 'Printed Page' kindly donated a copy of Cole's map of 1805. Many people have contributed by their written works and specialist knowledge, in particular Anthony Caesar, Utrick Casebourne, Gavin Edgerley-Harris, Derek Keene, Pamela Peskett, Edward Roberts, Philippa Stevens and Austin Whitaker, and to them I express my thanks.

John Crook not only took the 'now' photographs in 1992 and many of the copy photographs, but also gave freely of his considerable expertise in all matters relating to photography and to Winchester. Without his help the project could never have been completed.

Samantha Beasley, Ann Bailey and Lyn Stevens contributed much in their various ways in checking facts and inputting data, which has undoubtedly much improved the final product. The errors must, however, remain my responsibility alone.

My family have been enormously supportive and have allowed me the time and space to carry this project through in one of the busiest years to date.

Then and Now

So far as general pictures and maps of the city are concerned, Speed's map of *c.*1611 gives a helpful bird's eye view of Winchester in the 17th century, but pictures of Winchester begin to appear in reasonable numbers only in the 18th century.

The pictures in this first group are both historic and new. They show change wrought on the city by time, and its continual evolution; for example, the cathedral tower appears shrouded in scaffolding and largely cleared of it at different times during the summer of 1992 (illustrations 6 and 10). All the modern pictures were specially commissioned at this time and were taken during the course of the summer and autumn. The photographer, John Crook, has succeeded in giving the flavour of the city today. He shows its modern lightness and airiness, but also the larger scale of the 19th- and 20th-century structures, the impact of the motorcar, and the rather curious emptiness which pedestrianisation and the disappearance of residents from the centre of the city has brought about. This openness includes both city and close, as clearance of the outer close, west of the cathedral, has made a grassy sward today in contrast to the crooked tombstones and iron railings of a century ago (illustrations 9 and 10). Each of the pictures has been as far as possible taken from precisely the same spot as its predecessor, in some cases at the risk of life and limb to the photographer!

Apart from some variations the city had a comparatively high population from late Saxon times until the century leading up to the Reformation in the mid-16th century, with perhaps, on recent estimates, as many as 11,000 inhabitants for much of the period. In the two centuries following 1540, Reformation, Civil War and the final loss of royal status on the death of Charles II in 1688, led to the decline in population until there were perhaps as few as 4,000 inhabitants in the 18th century. Today within the city and suburbs there are some 30,000 people.

The timber and stone buildings of the middle ages and early modern period, and the great brick buildings of the 17th and 18th centuries, were joined in the 19th century by more red-brick work, this time terraced cottages and tenement buildings, many of which have now disappeared. To supply the growing population the commercial centre of the city grew, and there are many commercial and industrial premises built during the 19th century that can still be seen in the High Street and elsewhere. Commercial premises have characterised 20th-century building also, especially since the Second World War. Notable examples from recent times are found in St George's Street, where Sir Hugh Casson and Partners designed some colonnaded shops in 1962-5 in the then fashionable blue-brick, and in the Brooks Centre completed in 1991. Other notable, and even larger, structures have been the Hampshire County Council offices, originally designed in the 1930s, but not begun until the late 1950s. The County Record Office (illustration 32) will add to this remarkable stock.

Corner sites are amongst the most valuable and in this section a number are considered, showing how the increased demand for space has led to the destruction of many old buildings as leases have expired and landlords, often institutions, have built on a larger scale and changed the rôle of the buildings. Public houses and hotels in particular have suffered heavily in these developments in the search for better returns on capital investment.

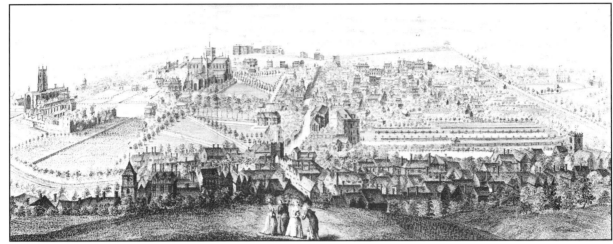

1 & 2. The Buck panorama of 1736 cannot be easily matched by a modern photograph because recent tree growth obscures the view. However, the southern half of the city can be seen. Many of the great buildings of the middle ages — cathedral, college, the Wolvesey Palace, home of the bishop, the royal castle hall, and St John's buildings in the Broadway are all plain to see in 1736 together with a number of timber-framed houses of the later middle ages. In the foreground on the left, beside St Peter's, Chesil, is the fine house once occupied by Sir Thomas Fleming, recorder of Winchester, who presided over the trial of the conspirators of the Gunpowder Plot in 1605-6. The main post-medieval structures are the great houses built during the campaigns associated with Charles II's proposed palace which commands the skyline. Bridge House (Mildmay House), the mansion which dominated the eastern end of the city, is still very much in evidence, together with Pescod's great Abbey House on the site of St Mary's nunnery, while in St Peter's Street, St Swithun's Street, on Castle Hill, at Hyde, and elsewhere in the city, great brick houses sprang up for the nobility. Further brick mansions such as Serle's House in Southgate Street seen just to the right of the cathedral (illustration 1) appeared in the 18th century.

3. Middle Brook Street (illustrations 4, 5 and 6) has changed as much as anywhere in the city and is chosen here as a small case study. This picture of Samuel Prout's watercolour of 1813 shows one of the brooks, which give the area its name, still open in the middle of the street. The entrance to Silver Hill is seen immediately to the right of the fishing group and old St Maurice's church in the High Street can be seen in the distance.

4. Late in the 19th century nos. 8, 9 and 10 (white between the framing) Middle Brook Street, survivors of medieval Winchester, are still recognisable as the buildings on the right in Prout's painting. Some of the buildings Prout shows have been replaced by 19th-century houses infilling between the older houses. William Winkworth, a chimney sweep, was at no. 8 in the 1880s and '90s; next to the *Duke of Wellington* which was at no. 9 until *c*.1909.

5. Looking south towards the cathedral along Middle Brook Street, towards the end of the 19th century. The jettied timber-framed buildings can be seen beyond the street lamp on the right. New St Maurice's, of which only the tower survives beside Debenham's today, is dominated by the cathedral. On the whole the census entries for this street in the 19th century do not number the properties, but refer only to the 'tenement' when listing the occupants.

6. As the cathedral tower begins to emerge from the scaffolding which has shrouded it recently, the post office building on the left, dating from *c*.1970, has been joined by the new Brooks Centre on the right. The timber-framed buildings have been demolished. Trees have apparently been planted over the long-since channelled brook. St Maurice's has given way to the red-brick of Debenham's, flat-roofed to give maximum space inside while preserving the view of the cathedral.

7. When this picture was taken in 1953, St George's, one of the narrow Saxon streets, had been built up with warehouses, such as Curnow's (demolished 1970) on the corner with St Peter's Street, and stores. The corner of Marks & Spencer's can just be seen on the left, with its winch above. One of Habel's furniture shops is seen on the right: it was demolished later in 1953.

8. The new Brooks Centre of 57 units, was completed in 1991 and now dominates the northern side of St George's Street, which has been considerably widened as can be seen in this 1992 photograph.

9. The west end of the cathedral and part of the Outer Close in 1882, before the tomb stones and railings were cleared and 'the ground lowered' as we learn from Thomas Stopher's album from which this is taken (illustration 17).

10. In this 1992 view there is not a tomb stone to be seen, except for the bases of the two war memorials visible below the trees. This is a popular area to lie on a sunny day during a burst of summer sunshine. However, some of the Winchester dead still lie undisturbed just below the surface, in contrast to the still-fenced cathedral green where they were disinterred in the 1960s.

11. A winter view looking westwards up the High Street *c.*1910. *The Plume of Feathers* was demolished in 1938, but traffic continued to use the Westgate for another 25 years or so.

12. Today a seemingly endless snake of traffic creeps down the hill. The corner of the county council's new Mottisfont Court building which contains Trading Standards offices, the council's information centre and shop is seen on the extreme right. Extensive repairs to the Westgate are under way: the removal of the ivy revealed further structural problems.

13. *The Star Inn* seen here *c*.1885 was situated at 83 High Street, on the corner of Staple Gardens. It was one of a number of timber-framed buildings in the city, with façades from a later period which were designed to give some additional ground floor space by taking in the area below the first floor jetties — and no doubt thereby encroaching somewhat on the highway.

14. The replacement building is much more roomy with an extra storey and extensive attic rooms: a more radical response to shortage of space. Formerly *The Talbot Inn*, successor to *The Star* by 1929, it was converted some years ago into estate agents' offices. Excavations for the cellars of the new building revealed several cists and skeletons in the squatting position, now believed to date from the Iron Age or Saxon period.

15. Looking down the hill past the junctions of Southgate Street and Jewry Street, immediately east of 83 High Street (illustration 13) in the 1920s. The *Black Swan Hotel*, demolished in the 1930s is a major loss. It was here, we are told, that Sherlock Holmes met Miss Hunter, the terrified nanny in *The Adventure of the Copper Beeches*. Indeed Conan Doyle, a keen photographer, may have known the hotel at first hand for it advertised photographic darkroom facilities. Perhaps he stayed there during his ghost hunting expeditions to Christchurch Priory. Another major loss is the *George Hotel,* demolished in 1956 to enable the widening of Jewry Street in order to cope with the increase in traffic at this major crossroads in the city.

16. In 1974 the flow of traffic east-west was diverted by the pedestrianisation of the High Street. One of the city's less successful blocks, the new Black Swan Buildings, has replaced the old hotel. Across the road is architect Owen Carter's unusual Egyptian-influenced corner building of *c.*1835 occupied by Hayward, with a shop front by Thomas Stopher (illustrations 17 and 18). Now, with a modern shop front, it is occupied by the Halifax Building Society. The bow-windowed Woolwich office on the left is a survivor. The signs on the neighbouring property hint at the difficulties experienced by businesses in the city in the 1990s — Winchester having been dubbed in the 1980s the wealthiest city in Britain.

17. Thomas Stopher, mayor, builder, architect and historian of Winchester was responsible for a number of developments in the city, often on corner sites, such as *The Green Man* on Southgate Street and St Swithun's Street. Here we see the old *Dolphin Inn*, on the corner of High Street and St Thomas's Street before 1880.

18. Stopher's large replacement building remained a public house until the hundred years of the lease was up. The building was then gutted, and now struggles for tenants in hard times. Alcohol, for home consumption, is still available on the site, from Oddbins.

19. *The Crown and Cushion Inn* seen here *c*.1900, was another of Stopher's corner developments and was situated on the corner of Jewry Street and North Walls, near the site of the old Northgate. Batchellor, a confectioner, whose cart is seen outside the inn, was at 130 High Street (illustration 23) for at least 40 years until the end of the First World War.

20. Stopher Stophered! The *Crown Hotel* was demolished in the 1980s to be replaced by Crown Walk, a building partly designed to allow access through to North Walls without the necessity of passing the dangerous corner. Amongst the current occupiers are the Country Gentlemen's Association, and the Redland Roofing Company. The handcart has given way to the Volvo, the open road to a thicket of traffic signs.

21. North Walls looking east when St Swithun's school was located in the street at the turn of the century. A safe enough place for horses, carts and children.

22. North Walls, today, during a lull in the welter of one-way traffic. Uncertainty about development plans and the incessant traffic have blighted the area, but a number of shops including two Chinese takeaways survive (*see* picture 29).

23. This scene, taken before 1900, would have been familiar to Mr. Batchellor, the confectioner (illustration 19), whose shop is visible here with the eye of faith, nine doors along from *The Suffolk Arms Inn* (known before 1880 as *The Marquis of Granby*). The public house was run successively by the Guy family in the 1880s, Mr. Page until 1896 and then by Edwin Blake until 1906. This photograph has been rescued from a most unpromisingly faded original with great skill.

24. The old public house on this prime site was displaced by Marks & Spencer's, managed by J. F. H. Kemp, in 1935. Such sites are now valued on the basis of the number of people who pass by, and by such a yardstick this crossroads, between the cathedral to the south, the post office to the north and the High Street running east-west up the hill, is amongst the prime sites in the city. Over the years M & S have expanded up the road beyond *The Suffolk Arms* site. Further up the precinct, on the corner of Market Street, at 25 High Street is Ratner's the jeweller, one of a number of jewellers clustered in that area of the High Street — H. Samuel at 27, and Ernest Jones across the road at 123-4, are all part of the Ratner Group.

25. Beyond the Eastgate bridge is the corner of Bridge Street and Chesil Street, seen here in 1905 about to be transformed by the demolition of Kelsey's and the adjacent property, early sacrifices to road widening schemes. Thomas Stopher kept a meticulous record of the development and history of properties, no doubt partly for business purposes, and so his albums in the City Museum and the Hampshire Record Office are an unrivalled source of information for the century up to his death, c.1930. He has written valuations below the photograph in his album of these properties, (*from left to right*) at £995, £550 and £575 for the Old Chesil Rectory (*right*).

26. The Old Chesil Rectory in 1992, provides almost the only reference point today. The Rectory was restored in 1892 and re-roofed in 1960. Behind, in the Chesil station yard, a multi-storey car park and an office development have sprung up in the 1980s.

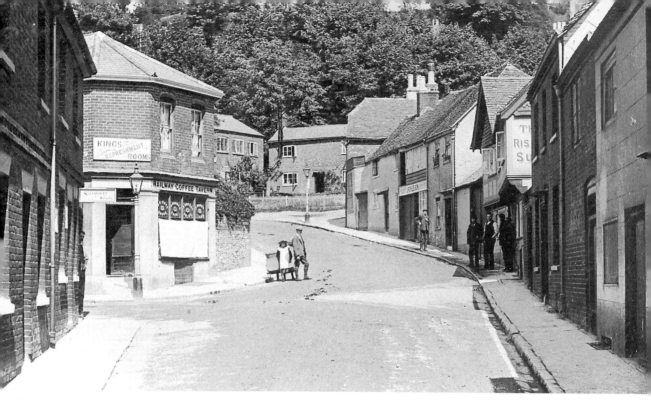

27. The adjacent railway (*see* illustrations 60 and 61) was no doubt the inspiration for The Railway Coffee Tavern. Ivy, who sent this card to Mr. Rose of Alderholt, Salisbury, *c*.1910, worked in the tavern, which she describes as 'our shop'. The building with the hipped gable beyond *The Rising Sun* was the premises from 1861 to 1922 of Richard Goodall, clay tobacco pipe maker, who had a pipe kiln in his garden.

28. Today, the houses on the left and on the right, forground, have been demolished, and the refreshment rooms, having latterly been Ken's Fish and Chip Shop, have recently been developed into residential accommodation. In these health-conscious times the clay tobacco pipe maker's premises are now a homeopathic clinic.

29. Outside the Eastgate to the north-east of the city lies the village of Winnall. Its church, St Martin's, was a medieval structure rebuilt in 1858 by William Coles 'with some old materials', presumably from its predecessor. Unlike other extra-mural churches which have survived better than their intra-mural brothers, St Martin's was demolished in the 1960s with an eye perhaps to the proposal, then popular, for a road link from the bypass to the centre of the city down Easton Lane, with a dual carriageway up North Walls. Despite the considerable antiquity of Winnall, which has yielded significant Saxon finds, there was no excavation undertaken on this site.

30. The same view today is almost unrecognisable apart from the steep hollow way of Easton Lane, and the curve of the access road off to the right. The church lay just inside what is now the main industrial area of the city, the Winnall Industrial Estate. Not surprisingly a great deal of preparatory work was necessary to locate the exact area to enable this photograph to be taken.

31. On the corner of Sussex Street and Station Hill, outside the north-west corner of the historic defences stood the *Carfax Hotel*. Situated near the main railway station, the hotel flourished until *c*.1960, before it fell into disrepair. It was then put to a variety of uses including, for a time, a student residence (reputedly haunted by ghosts) for King Alfred's College, before being scheduled for demolition in connection with the Central Area Traffic Plan in August 1971.

32. In 1992 the new Hampshire Record Office was nearing completion on part of the site formerly occupied by the *Carfax Hotel* and adjacent properties. The rest of the site has since been engulfed by road widening. Excavations revealed remains of what appeared to have been a hawkhouse of the medieval kings, and huge early ditches. A truly historic place to gather up the magnificent archives of Winchester and Hampshire.

33. Canon Street lies outside the southern wall of the medieval city, parallel to St Swithun's Street which is within the walls. The remains of the walls are to be found incorporated into the shared garden walls which run between the two streets. This picture looking west was taken before 1893 when *The Rose and Crown* ceased to operate.

34. A century later and little has changed, superficially — a bricked up doorway here, a rebuilt façade there, dormers demolished or reshaped, a door hood, no doubt wrecked by a passing lorry, replaced. However, economically, demographically and socially Canon Street could hardly be more different. Apart from *The Wykeham Arms*, other public houses have vanished as have commercial premises such as Ann Shergold's grocery business and the shop on the corner of St Swithun's Villas. The mix of business and residential property has almost vanished, as have the children, for the cottages in Canon Street are no longer in demand as family houses. The brothels which, according to tradition, kept this street out of bounds to College boys, have also disappeared.

Celebrating Winchester's Past

Winchester's rich medieval royal and ecclesiastical heritage needs little introduction. Recent work has done much to clarify the rôle of the Romans, the Saxon and medieval kings, bishops, institutions and the daily life of the city. Post-medieval Winchester remains much less known despite the surge of interest in urban history during the last couple of decades. This is partly due to the lack of a full and published catalogue of records either for the city or for the diocese. However, major projects are now underway to prepare these publications and research on Winchester will be much facilitated by their appearance. In addition a project is in progress to prepare a building-by-building survey of the city in order to give the history of business and occupation between 1550 and the present day and to unite pictorial and documentary evidence.

Archaeological work in the city has been second to none in Europe in the last 30 years or so, and the meticulously prepared publications arising from the remarkable series of excavations between 1961 and 1971 are beginning to appear. Recent volumes give details of thousands of medieval archaeological finds in the city, from tools and furnishings to musical instruments and games. Museums have been established in the city for well over a century, but are desperately in need of major new premises to display the finds which fill warehouses all over Winchester. Such major displays would no doubt draw even larger throngs to the ancient capital.

The people of Winchester have long enjoyed a strong sense of identity with their city's past. The history which brings tens of thousands of visitors to the city each year has been fostered by mayors, councillors, institutions and individuals with the interests of the city at heart. For example, Mayor Bowker saw the millenary celebrations of Alfred in 1901, Barbara Carpenter Turner, a more recent mayor, has ceaselessly investigated various aspects of the city's history, sharing her researches through many successful lecture series, newspaper articles and the most substantial history of the city this century; and Pamela Peskett as well as carrying through a large amount of research herself, gave priority to historical study of Winchester during her mayoralty by making research into the city one of the foci of her mayoral charities. Councillor and Mrs. Neate supported the excavations in the 1960s and gave much of their own money towards the resulting publications. Town officials such as Charles Bailey in 1856, people from the educational establishments, such as J. S. Furley from Winchester College in the 1920s and Tom Atkinson from King Alfred's College, who wrote a history of Elizabethan Winchester in the 1960s, have all made contributions. The most detailed study to date has been that of the medieval city, published by Derek Keene in 1985.

There has been a number of major celebrations of the city's past since the millenary celebrations of 1901. In 1908 a great pageant was held to raise funds for restoration of the cathedral. Completion of the repairs was marked in great style with a royal visit in 1912 (illustration 185). The 800th anniversary of the foundation of St Cross by Henry of Blois occurred in 1936. In 1979 the 900th anniversary of the foundation of the cathedral was celebrated by further processions around the city and many other events. The 1980s saw the 600th anniversary of the foundation of Winchester College; 1990 the 150th anniversary of the foundation of the training college since 1928 King Alfred's College. The year 2000 will be the 900th anniversary of the burial of William II (Rufus) at Winchester, and 2007 will be the 800th anniversary of the birth of King Henry III in the city.

35 & 36. For some five centuries the Round Table has hung on the wall of the Great Hall of the castle. Since at least 1873, when it was taken down, as seen here, there has been no doubt that it was a table as the mortices from which the legs were roughly removed can be seen. Suggested dates for its construction range from the time of Edward I (d.1307), who reburied Arthur's remains at Glastonbury, to Edward III (d.1377), who founded an order of the Round Table in homage to Arthur in 1344. It was probably painted (note the Tudor rose) in 1522 for the visit of Emperor Charles V. The bearded King Arthur — thoroughly cleaned and restored since this picture was taken — may well be Henry VIII, the Emperor's host. Henry's elder brother Arthur had been christened at Winchester with great pomp in 1486, to give the Tudors a spurious aura of antiquity. All are agreed that the table does not date back to King Arthur's time.

37 & 38. It was decided in 1898, at a national meeting of interested parties, to celebrate the millennium of Alfred's death in 1901, two years too late by modern reckoning. Alfred Bowker the indefatigable mayor who had first raised the idea in 1897 saw the project through with great panache. Hamo Thornycroft was engaged as the sculptor and his plaster model was cast in bronze and raised on a mighty plinth of Cornish granite. This picture shows the statue about to be raised onto the plinth. However, disaster struck and the two men undertaking the operation were injured when the poles supporting the winch gave way. The exercise was then delayed by six weeks, while the men recovered in hospital. Eventually, amidst great celebrations, the statue was unveiled.

39 & 40. In 1906 it was discovered that the cathedral was in critical danger of collapsing, which led to the city holding a National Pageant in 1908 to raise money. This celebrated occasion represented key figures and events from the city's history. Here we see the Rev. E. Macpherson dressed as the Duke of Normandy (William I) and Mr. J. A. Fort as William of Wykeham.

41. Spanish stately dancers, part of the group recalling Queen Mary's marriage in the cathedral to Philip of Spain in 1554. The commemorative pageant was aimed at raising national consciousness concerning the plight of the cathedral and to raise funds to enable the structure to be underpinned and buttressed (illustrations 147-50).

42. In 1936, St Cross Hospital celebrated the 800th anniversary of its original foundation by Bishop Henry of Blois. Here, Bishop Garbett (1932-42) and a choir assemble outside the hall ready to proceed to the church.

43. The meeting of the British Archaeological Institute in the St John's Rooms in 1845 was a notable event. The 'assembly room', decorated with festoons and oval mirrors, together with portraits including Lely's *Charles II* (now in the Guildhall), provided a splendid setting. Hundreds visited and were treated to papers by the antiquarian Titans of the day including Professor Willis (on the cathedral), Sir Thomas Phillipps, J. G. Nichols and T. H. Turner. This meeting perhaps more than any other event provided a touchstone for studies of the historical and architectural remains of the medieval city and its environs, an interest which continues unabated to this day.

44. Winchester's archaeological heritage began to attract more attention as the 20th century progressed. One of the pioneers was Sydney Ward-Evans, affectionately known as Winchester's 'honorary archaeologist' from 1926 until his death in 1943. He is shown here demonstrating the width of castle walls revealed in pre-war excavation. Excavations in the 1950s and 1960s were led by Barry Cunliffe and subsequently by Martin Biddle, both now of Oxford University. Martin Biddle's excavations lasted over ten years from 1961-71 and principally laid open the site of the Old Minster, part of the castle, large areas of Wolvesey and a residential area in the Brooks. The excavations were supported by a major campaign of documentary research. Since the 1970s the fieldwork has been amplified by the efforts of the Winchester Archaeology Office under Ken Qualmann.

45. Members of the group representing characters from the history of the city which gathered in 1979 to celebrate the 900th anniversary of the foundation of the cathedral. Those seen here outside 11 The Close include (*from left to right*) Walter Raleigh (Philip Ray), Henry of Blois (Paul Ranger), Rufus (Ian Crowe), Walkelin (Richard Warner), Emma (Annette Williams), Cnut (Martin Doughty) and Aethelwold (John Marshall).

46. The same occasion. Tim Hart Dyke as Freddie Frost the cyclist in The Square, almost outside the Frosts' former premises (illustration 68).

Civic Government and Public Services

Winchester has never been in the forefront of municipal reform. Although it gained a number of charters it never obtained county status, as did Southampton by 1450, and Winchester government continued in its same old ways. In the 19th century, franchise reforms encouraged the city to put its political house in order. The 1974 local government reorganisation made a major impact with the extension of Winchester to include its district hinterland. This was a completely new venture, and considerably reduced the powers of the city councillors who now had no majority in the district. In recent years the local struggle between Conservatives and Liberals has been a close one within the district. On the whole the city has been more Liberal (and radical with a small number of Labour councillors) whilst the countryside has remained more Conservative.

The functions of local government administration have continued to dominate the city with education and local finance offices. The courts have seen many famous trials on occasion followed by executions or custodial sentences. A number of prisons have been built including the County Bridewell at Hyde to the north of the city (*see* endpaper), the great jail in Jewry Street (1805), which still stands, and finally the new 19th-century star-shaped prison built by 1850 on the West Hill, outside the formerly walled area of the city, near the Romsey Road.

Plaster casts of the faces of hanged men, used in the 19th century for now discredited phrenological purposes, are preserved in the City Museum. Amongst the hideously distorted features it can be seen that ethnic origins and mental illness may have contributed to the choice of casts.

47. An 1818 view looking south along Jewry Street, here called Gaol Street, towards the High Street taken from Ball's *Walks*, a series of maps and text designed to show the ancient city to the visitor on foot. This illustration shows two major buildings at that time, namely the theatre (on the left), and the prison designed by George Moneypenny and completed *c.*1805. One bay of the theatre survived until *c.*1980 when during the course of building work on the adjacent former garage site the remaining bay mysteriously collapsed. Vigilant officials required its rebuilding and a modern version can be seen today. The prison has managed to survive, although it operated as a prison for a comparatively short time until the new and much larger prison was completed on the West Hill.

48. It is known that the pioneer photographer Fox Talbot worked in Winchester, although it is not known who took this early photograph, *c*.1850, which shows the town pump near the Buttercross, or City Cross. The communal pump brings to mind the serious problems which beset towns before adequate water supplies were available: sewage all too frequently contaminated the water. The Cross was erected in Cardinal Beaufort's time in the 15th century, and is 43 feet high. This picture shows it between the repairs of 1835, and the major restoration of 1865. Sarah Wooldridge's butcher's shop occupied the corner of the Pentice. Thomas Stopher, writing in *c*.1913, recalled meeting a man who worked in the only other butcher's shop in town in Wooldridge's time which was also run by a woman. Stopher's informant told him that the two ladies bought a bullock each week and shared it half each, and that this was the only meat eaten in the city. A print by Owen Carter *c*.1840 shows meat hanging in Mrs. Wooldridge's window. The census of 1841 records that Mrs. Wooldridge's elder sons, who may have been twins, did not follow their mother into the butcher's trade, but instead became a printer and a banker's clerk. By 1871 Mary Tanner, printer and stationer, and her eight children were in residence. This picture may represent an intermediate stage as it is clearly not a butcher's shop, and a sign which may read 'Tanner' can be made out at the top of the shop window.

49. In 1873 the vacant area adjacent to the Broadway and Abbey House (illustration 1) was filled by the great neo-Gothic Guildhall designed by Jeffery and Skiller in celebration of Winchester's Gothic heritage. Emulating the style of the great Cloth Hall at Ypres, Belgium, the Guildhall was completed in its initial phase in 1873. To the west, a School of Art was built on the site of the former police station.

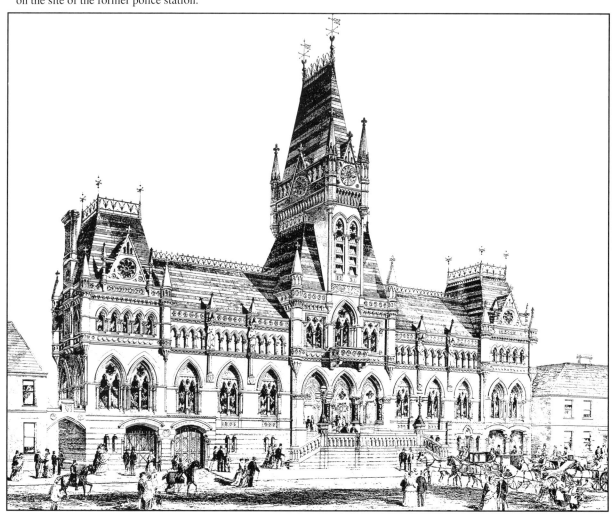

50. The Garnier Road pumping station, opened in 1875, overcame the problems of sewage disposal which had plagued the city since the middle ages. Dean Garnier, who gave his name to the building and the road in which it was built, was a noted philanthropist and would no doubt be delighted to be recalled by a sewage works. Sewage disposal in the city is still a major issue with current provision on the northern slopes of St Catherine's Hill, as inhabitants are reminded when the wind is in the east. The coming of the road through Twyford Down is forcing new provision, which should remove the cause of the smell.

51. This 1883 picture from Thomas Stopher's album shows the corporation assembled in front of Alderman Fielder's house. Stopher himself is the bareheaded man behind the mayor, and on his left is T. F. Kirby, another historically-minded member of the corporation.

52. A view of the long-vanished Anglican Chapel in the West Hill Cemetery designed by Owen Carter (d.1859). His gate lodge, once surmounted by a bell cote, still survives. Plans kept at the Heritage Centre, Upper Brook Street, show that most of Winchester's population through several generations were buried here. Amongst the many graves can be seen those of Mayor Richard Moss, a philanthropic brewer, the musician William Whiting (d.1878), composer of 'Eternal Father Strong to Save', and an obelisk, erected by fellow pugilists, to the memory of Charles Freeman (d.1843), the 'American Giant' who died suddenly whilst visiting Winchester. There are also many military graves, see the section 'Wartime and Military Matters' below. The majority of memorials in the cemetery has now been destroyed.

53. After the erection of the statue in 1901, these firemen with their 1889 Merryweather steamer 'Victoria' appear to be giving Alfred a wash — possibly to remove the sugar (which melted in the heat), reportedly used to slide the statue into place. 'Victoria' was scrapped in 1917. The Brigade Captain in the picture is J. A. Sawyer, standing in front of the statue, with brass helmet and epaulets.

Convict's Escape from Winchester Goal.

Major Richardson & Bloodhounds.

54. In late April 1909 a Belgian convict called Witer escaped from Winchester 'goal', as this hastily printed commemorative card calls it. Major Richardson of Harrow and his trained bloodhounds were summoned and joined the chase. The escapee was eventually recaptured near Leckford in the Test Valley by mounted police, after he had spent 84 hours on the run.

55. 1913. The Judge for the Winchester Assizes and his escort of policemen assemble in the Broadway complete with truncheons. The police station by this time was located in the east end of the adjacent Guildhall. The uniformed coachmen on the High Sheriff's coach can just be seen below the statue.

56. A postcard taken by the celebrated Winchester photographer, Charles Beloe, of the 'Union Infirmary' (illustration 88). It reminds us of the link in Winchester, as elsewhere, between the workhouse and the old people's hospital — St Paul's as it has been known since the end of the Second World War. In the 1930s as the Winchester Union, 1 St Paul's Hill, it still included a 'Labour Master' as the senior official after the master and matron.

57. Fireman William Bell's funeral in March 1934. He was buried in West Hill Cemetery. Bell, who lived at 3 Tower Street, was a painter by trade and was taken ill while working at the hospital. Two of his sons became firemen at the time of his death. Bell's father was the master of the Bombay Hounds for nearly twenty years. William Bell was an enthusiastic cricketer, singer and member of the Hampshire Militia.

58. Central to Winchester's role as a 19th-century market town was the Corn Exchange in Jewry Street (now the City Library). Designed by Owen Carter in the popular Italianate style of the mid-19th century, its portico was probably modelled on that of Inigo Jones's St Paul's in Covent Garden, London, whilst the fashionable yellow brick imitates Prince Albert's Osborne House. Between the wars, as seen here, the building was used as a 'picture theatre' with restaurant, and as a function hall. Adjacent is *The Market Inn*, which may also have been designed by Carter, now The Theatre Royal — a third location for a theatre in Jewry Street, although The Theatre Royal has been a cinema for most of its existence.

59. Queen Elizabeth Court, as it was to become, was designed in the 1930s, as this picture by the architect C. Cowles Voysey shows, but was not built until 1959-60, 'entirely untouched by the last 30 years of architecture' (Nikolaus Pevsner). The Queen visited in 1959 to declare the building officially open. The additional arch beside the Westgate and the impressive entrance steps were never built.

Transport

Winchester owes its primary road form to the Romans, but the pattern of Roman streets was lost and forgotten when the Saxons relaid the grid *c*.900. The new arrangements included a network of small 'service streets', exemplified by St George's Street which remained in its narrow form until *c*.1960, when it was widened, and St Clement's Street which is still narrow today. Both these streets lie parallel to the High Street (*see* endpapers and frontispiece). Another feature of the Saxon layout is the partial circuit of streets which lie within the walls, St Swithun's Street being a notable example. The demands of traffic led first to the demolition of the city gates, with the exception of the Westgate, which only narrowly escaped destruction, whilst the obsolescence of the walls allowed for the opening up of roads such as North Walls.

Road and rail depots, and industrial works grew up near the sites of the former gates to ease communication. A plan to site the main railway station within the ancient walls in the north-west quarter of the city was only just defeated. Even so, much of the archaeology associated with the entrance to the castle from the west beyond the walls, disappeared in the creation of the railway cutting which now runs from St James's Lane to Romsey Road. The Chesil station of the Didcot, Newbury and Southampton Junction line (from 1923 Great Western Railway, and 1948 British Railways) was located not far from the site of the former Eastgate. By the site of the Southgate lay Parker's stables and hackney depot. Nearby a brewery could be seen, one of a number scattered round the periphery of the circuit of the medieval town area: at St James's Lane, St Swithun's Street, Eastgate Street and most notably in Hyde Street beyond the site of the Northgate, which is the only brewery remains of which have survived.

Hackney carriages and horse-drawn drays gave way to mechanical transport, both commercial and private. A notable first in private motoring was the purchase in August 1897 of a Coventry-built Daimler. General H. P. Montgomery of Southgate Street, the proud owner of the car, was the first private person in the country who was unconnected with the motor industry to possess an English made car. He died in 1901 and was buried in the West Hill Cemetery. Bus companies flourished in the city, notably the King Alfred Motor Services which began early in the 1920s running a service to the new estate at Stanmore. Others followed, notably the Hants and Dorset Motor Services Ltd. with their 'Omnibus Station' (illustration 192), built in a yard accessed through the northern side of the Broadway in the 1930s. For many the advent of the private motor car made little difference, and they continued to use the buses and trains. Bicycles were very popular and the city had a long tradition of bicycle sale and repair premises until recently, when the Chesil cycle shop, relocated in North Walls, closed.

The main artery of the city remains the High Street, now largely pedestrianised. No doubt motor traffic has blighted certain streets which were formerly more prosperous, by making them especially difficult for pedestrians to cross. Examples of this are Jewry Street, north of the junction with St George's Street, and St George's Street itself as the empty premises and frequently changing tenancies show (*see* illustrations 21 and 22).

Strenuous efforts are being made at present to remove as much traffic as possible from the city. Current arrangements enable traffic to get into the centre from the four corners, but force it out the same way due to a lack of through ways. This causes great difficulties for visitors, who also find it hard to park. A park and ride scheme is being proposed, but there is some ambivalence towards this from the business community. Time will tell!

60 & 61. The London and South Western Railway station had already been a feature of the Winchester landscape for almost 50 years, when the Didcot, Newbury and Southampton Junction Railway opened their Chesil station in 1885. The extension across the meadows to Shawford followed six years later, no doubt delayed by engineering difficulties. The picture above shows the digging (or 'farming' as Stopher calls it — presumably in the dialect sense of emptying) of the cutting south towards St Catherine's Hill, for the new Chesil station. Picture 61 shows the crowds which turned out to see the first train to Newbury on 4 May 1885.

62. The new D.N.S.J.R. station at 3 Chesil Street, around the turn of the century.

63. The L.S.W.R. station *c.*1900 after it had been remodelled perhaps in response to the D.N.S.J.R. challenge. All the buildings, other than the station and those on Stockbridge Road (*right*), have now disappeared.

64. George Parker's stables and hackney depot occupied this site on Southgate Street from c.1880-1917. Subsequently Will Short's garage, the premises are now Short's Peugeot garage. When a showroom was under construction in the 1930s on a site immediately to the right of this picture, remains of the Roman and medieval Southgate were discovered. On the left can be seen the chimney of the brewery in St James's Lane, the cellars of which survived until they were filled in when Southgate Villas were built c.1980.

65. Bill Passey and his trap, the sort of vehicle which could have been hired from Parker's, outside a nicely diapered house in Lower Brook Street, early in the century.

66. At the millenary celebrations in 1901 a traction engine was needed to move the great Cornish stones for the statue's plinth from the railway to the Broadway. Here the procession is shown passing 105 High Street, now the National Westminster Bank.

67. Various pictures survive of the crash of this Daimler at St Cross on 8 June 1908. This one was taken the following morning. The remains of the cart demolished by the motor car emphasise the old and new transport in use at that period. The accident occurred after 11 p.m. when Mr. Farquhar of London, accompanied by his valet and chauffeur, was hurrying south to catch the Le Havre ferry at Southampton. One theory as to the cause was that the car, zig-zagging to avoid the signpost to Twyford located in the middle of the road at Ghost Corner, went out of control and struck Mr. Salter's cart which was returning from the Royal Counties Show at Southampton. Five people were taken to hospital.

68. Gale and Verrall's shop at 159 High Street as it appeared in their advertisement in *Warren's Directory* of 1909. The premises now appear to be The Broadway Shop. Despite the hills, Winchester had an enthusiastic cycling fraternity before the First World War, which included an élite Cycling Corps in the Hampshire Volunteers. Mr. Sharland made the city's very own 'Winton' cycle at his shop at 24 Jewry Street around the turn of the century. All this may have been inspired by the success of Freddie Frost, Wintonian cycling champion who trained *c*.1895 in the cellar of Frost's watchmaking business, now the London Camera Exchange, in The Square.

69. A photograph of Mr. Clifford's cart by the Pentice in the High Street in October 1910. Clifford (on the right wearing a bowler hat) supplied many businesses including the shop opposite at 111 High Street whose produce is on display. It was called Jeffery & Son, florists and nurserymen, from 1892 until 1935, when it became Hepworths. Clifford had just sold all his produce when the picture was taken, prior to returning to Eastleigh.

70. The rural scene at Black Bridge, College Walk and Wharf Hill, was peaceful enough around the wharf of the canal. However, the heartfelt cry of the writer, in the summer of 1917, 'Oh for the war to be over so one can enjoy life', leaves no doubt about national and local preoccupations at the time this photograph was taken.

71. This Dennis lorry served the Water and Gas Company which as the Gaslight and Coke Company had been formed in 1847. The company was united with the Water Company following the Winchester Water and Gas Act of 1865. In 1936 it was split up again; Southampton took over the gas undertaking, Winchester retained water. The Winchester premises were behind Jewry Street, reached from Staple Gardens. Some of the old Gas Company buildings are still quite readily identifiable to the south of the library car park.

72. A bus driver from the King Alfred Company, with another Dennis vehicle en route to the Broadway, *c.*1930. The Chisnells ran this company for over half a century until it was taken over by the National Bus Company in 1973 when, according to the *Hampshire Chronicle*, the King Alfred Company was 'the last private bus company in England'.

73. The Winchester bypass around the time of its completion in the 1930s. At that time it was, according to the British Road Federation which published this picture, 'one of England's few modern roads'. The reader was urged to 'note the dual carriageway'. When the bypass was built there were no motorways in Britain to compare with those in America, let alone the motorways of France, Germany and Italy. How advanced it was then!

74. From the 1930s (or '40s), when this picture was taken, coach travellers became familiar with the Worthy Road coach station, conveniently sited near the London road. It went out of use *c*.1980 and became Flamingo Park, before development as the *Saxon Hotel* after 1985. Parts of the old structure are incorporated into the new. Since 1990 it has been the *Winchester Moat House Hotel*.

75. A picture taken towards the end of the life of the Chesil line, looking north to the tunnel under St Giles's Hill, with the station in a dilapidated state.

76. This photograph taken in the summer of 1959 shows a Collett 0-6-0 steaming towards the northern end of the Winchester loop at Winnall. Two years later passenger services were discontinued on the line, although oil and other freight services to the Midlands continued until 1965.

77. A Leyland TD2/1 built around 1950 going about its business probably in the 1960s. It was withdrawn from service in 1971. Beyond is a vehicle of the Greyfriars company of Winchester who were mainly coach operators. Prangnell the baker is still in the same premises as in 1908 (illustration 180), with Charles or Cecil (illustration 146) or their descendants in charge.

Living in Winchester

The great houses of Charles II's courtiers and their 18th-century successors (illustration 79) were joined by mass housing in the Brooks area of the city in the mid-19th century (illustration 96). From then onwards, with the space in the centre of the city filled once more, substantial housing sprang up at the margins of the medieval city. Examples of such houses include the Pagoda House and Medecroft to the south, and Kerrfield to the west. These properties to an extent were encouraged by the administrative development of the West Hill, also in the mid-19th century, by such institutions as the hospital and prison, which moved from within the walls. The north, south, east and west suburbs grew; more grand to the south in the Christchurch Road and St Cross area, less so at Highcliffe to the east or Hyde to the north. Terraces grew after 1880 along what was to become the Alresford Road, developing slowly up to the beginning of the First World War with a scatter of detached houses up the hill beyond St John's Road. Across the Alresford Road there were grander houses built on St Giles's Hill, many on land made available by the Baring family.

After the First World War there was much national debate about 'homes fit for heroes to live in' for those who had survived that holocaust, in which some 450 young men from the city gave their lives. But the heroes were not to have it all their own way: a national debate took place about whether or not the new housing should include a parlour, with all the potential subversion implied in such a term. In the end parlours were included, and fine, well built and well laid out estates appeared, notably at Stanmore which won a national prize for its excellence (illustration 94).

After the Second World War, the city grew rapidly, as farmland at Weeke, Harestock and at Teg Down was built over. Maps of the city show how frequently the modern layouts of these areas reflect the shapes of the fields they replaced. However, some corners of the city remained largely as they had been in the 18th century, especially The Close, although even there some changes have taken place, for example in the case of Canon Valpy's house, a quiet backwater at the turn of the century, which was put to other uses from the 1930s (illustrations 87 and 88).

78. *The Blue Boar* built on the corner of St John's Street and Blue Ball Hill, in the eastern suburb of the city, is amongst the oldest residential properties in Winchester and may date back to the 14th century. By 1774 it had ceased to function as an inn from which it derived its name. It has been much rebuilt, but retains a number of significant early features including a central galleried hall, open to the roof, with chambers at each end. Restoration was supervised by W. J. Carpenter Turner, cathedral architect (d.1981).

79. This view of the Westgate in the early 19th century shows just how bare of houses the area inside the gate had been since the end of the middle ages. In the 15th century there were buildings here on both sides of the High Street, but these had disappeared by 1650. Development began again in the 1830s. The Westgate itself was still an effective bar to entry with no pedestrian way on the south (left). A substantial section of the city wall can be seen to the north (right) which survived into this century (illustration 11).

80. Morley College almshouses were founded in 1672 by Bishop Morley and are on the north side of the cathedral in the outer close (front endpaper). The successors of the monks retained control of the southern, or inner, close which is still locked at night. This picture was taken before 1880 and shows the 17th-century buildings before they were rebuilt by John Colson, senior (d.1894). The scale of this rebuilding to the casual observer today is remarkably similar to Morley's original.

81. In 1851, as the nation enjoyed the Great Exhibition, *The Illustrated London News* carried this drawing of the 'cottage of the mayor of Southampton', a truly outlandish piece of architecture built near the junction of St James's Lane and Sparkford Road. Although the 'cottage' has lost (if it ever possessed) much of the ornament seen here, it survives in quite recognisable form as a brick, flint and ironwork structure. The 'Pagoda House', as it is familiarly known, has passed through a variety of uses, including being divided into small council bed-sits. It was rescued *c*.1970 and converted into a tutorial college by Peter Hitchin, before it became a private residence once more.

82. From the mid-19th century onwards, larger houses were built around the edge of the city as space within the walls dwindled. Medecroft was a typical example, built for J. N. Heale, M.D. (d.1891) in the shadow of the railway embankment on 20 acres of land bought from the Diocese in 1868. It had fields, a farm, a vinery and a tropical greenhouse which were sited on the west and north sides of the house. In 1882 three Bosvilles lived there, the oldest of them aged 22, and were served by five live-in servants. By 1904, it was put up for sale as a complete estate or as building plots, but was sold intact and occupied by Dame Emily Newdigate-Newdegate (d.1924), widow of a commander of the Rifle Brigade depot. The house was requisitioned in the Second World War for evacuees from the bombing in Southampton. In 1953 the house was converted into a prep school for St Swithun's, and is now home to the Archaeology and Art departments of King Alfred's College, shorn of almost all its land.

83. Kerrfield, occupied in the 1880s by Gordon Dewar, was further west on the Romsey Road, opposite Chilbolton Avenue which was created in 1912. The house can be seen here in its heyday *c*.1910, but was burnt out and left standing as a ruin for some years. In the early 1980s the site was redeveloped, together with that of the adjacent Melbury Lodge, a fine, shuttered Italianate building, and converted into high grade executive housing on the steep south-facing slopes of the Downs.

84. This picture was taken looking north, up Bar End Road, *c.*1910. No. 20, known as Barfield House in 1882, was occupied by the Fears and Miss Godwin, and is seen here on the left. Pullen's racing stables can be glimpsed beyond Barfield House also on the left. As elsewhere in the city, the tide of brick terracing flowed out along the approach roads. In 1928 the house was occupied by the Miss Fitts, and was demolished at that time.

Winchester Cottage Improvement Society, Limited.

OFFICE OF THE COMPANY,

19, St. Peter's Street, Winchester,

22 Dec 1896

I herewith send you the subjoined Statement and the Warrant annexed thereto for the amount of Dividend due on the Shares therein stated.

Your obedient Servant,

WALTER BAILEY, Secretary.

Dividend for the Half-year ending 30 Nov 1896, at the rate of 4 per cent. per Annum.

AMOUNT OF SHARES.	AMOUNT OF DIVIDEND.
£ 50	1 " "

85. Some development of small brick accommodation was financed by the Winchester Cottage Improvement Society, which returned a comfortable annual dividend in 1896. Property developed in this way includes Culverwell Gardens, off Culver Road, which will celebrate its centenary in the summer of 1994. The Society's sign today discourages non-resident parking in front of Culverwell Gardens, adjacent to Long Reign cottages, products of the period either side of 1890.

86. Many brick terraces were built in and around the city at the turn of the century. Arthur Road at Hyde, seen here c.1908, retains a uniform aspect and a rural flavour. Beloe the photographer was living in Arthur Road at this time, and the lady with the pushchair, who appears in other pictures by him, may have had some connection with him (illustration 179).

87. Canon Valpy's drawing room at 3 The Close *c*.1900. The canon was a man of independent means whose household included a number of servants and footmen. This picture is from a series of interiors of his house painted by B. O. Corfe at the end of Victoria's reign. It shows his fine sunny drawing room, such as would have been familiar to the clergy in Trollope's Barchester novels.

88. The house is now the Pilgrims' School, and the Canon's drawing room a sunny dormitory. The elegant porcelain and fine furniture have given way to Union Jack bedcovers, bears and other animals. The fireplace is as magnificent as ever.

89. The corner shop and post office in Lower Stockbridge Road, 1912. It was taken from the foot of the bridge by the up-line of the main station.

90. Fairfield Road, which dates from the mid-1890s, shows a diversity of development. In the process of attempting to build a variety of larger and smaller terraced houses, the developer bankrupted himself. This picture by Beloe shows the houses when they were about ten years old.

91. In Paternoster Row, by the east end of the cathedral, older properties remained in use, often crumbling as can be seen here. These ancient houses survived until they were cleared in 1960 to make way for city council offices and car parking facilities.

92. By the Kingsgate, seen here at the turn of the century, this shop and house flourished in a better state of repair, until they were demolished in the 1930s (illustration 100).

93. Probably early in the First World War, this rather mysterious picture of a group of women and babies on the steps of the Guildhall is captioned, 'Where may we live in Winchester?'. They are perhaps Belgian refugees, pictured as an element in the anti-German propaganda of those days, when all sorts of rumours about enemy atrocities were rife in England.

94 & 95. Stanmore was created after the Great War as part of a drive to provide adequate housing for the heroes who survived. Parlours were included here, and the model-village aspect of Stanmore and the good quality of the houses can still be seen today. After the Second World War things were not so good. The prefabs in the Valley at Stanmore were not so fine, but provided shelter for many families until they were finally demolished in the 1980s.

96. 1956. Looking out northwards over the Brooks, then filled with houses. The Ritz was one of three cinemas active in the city then. Holy Trinity church was very 'high' with processions and incense, and embellished by a remarkable series of wall paintings (illustration 145). This picture was taken from the back roof of the bus station (illustration 192).

School and College

Any account of education must begin with Winchester College, already in place by 1400, a tribute to Bishop Wykeham's enlightenment in a plague-ravaged country. Most of the schools in the city began as parish or denominational schools in the 19th century in response to the education acts. Some of these schools still perform their original function, such as St Faith's near St Cross, while others such as St John's (parish rooms), or St Michael's (architects' offices) have had to seek new rôles. Peter Symonds' College was opened as a school for boys aged 11 to 18 at 39 Southgate Street (the old judges' lodgings) in May 1897. It had moved to Owens Road by Christmas 1899.

Education for girls was developed at St Swithun's, first on the North Walls site, and latterly on a green field site to the east of the city. With the development of the Stanmore estate, facilities were provided there. In the leafy suburbs the County High, Henry Beaufort, their successors and additional primary schools have supplied the city's needs together with prep schools such as the Pilgrims' School and, until its recent closure, West Downs on the Romsey Road.

The Diocesan Training College was founded in 1840 and became King Alfred's College in 1928. The institution celebrated its 150th anniversary in 1990, a celebration held at a time of great expansion in numbers. Originally designed for 56 students, the college now caters for some 3,000. It has a significant impact on the city as the major institution of Higher Education, offering a broad range of studies to degree level, from archaeology and American studies to computing and Japanese studies, as well as providing for the training of teachers and degree courses for nurses. The School of Art in Park Avenue, although small in numbers, has also developed an excellent reputation.

97. This relaxed scene of cricket on Winchester College playing fields probably dates to before 1862, as the College tower in the background appears to be in the form in which it was completed *c*.1485. It was completely demolished and rebuilt in 1862 by the architect Butterfield, who undertook a number of commissions in the city at that time (illustration 141 and 157).

98. New facilities were apparently provided for racquet sports together with a new gymnasium *c*.1875-80 at Winchester College, perhaps designed by Stopher as this is taken from his album. All this to pursue that 'muscular Christianity' so popular amongst schoolmasters in the century after 1850.

99. The College masters in 1884, in the days of Ridding (*centre*), that most celebrated of Winchester heads. He gave way in that year to Dr. Fearon, who presided in 1887 over the 500th anniversary of the laying of the foundation stone.

100. College Street just before the First World War, as those who went to fight must have remembered it. Until the mid-1930s, buildings stood on the north side of the street at Laverty's Corner (illustration 92). By the Second World War they had become the gardens that are there today.

101. The Diocesan Training College as it was built in 1862 to designs by John Colson, senior. Colson's designs incorporated fashionable elements of Third Empire style. The Principal occupied a five-bedroomed house built at the east end (right) of the building, with a house for the deputy at the west end. The students' accommodation lay between, with lecture rooms on the ground floor. The original plans are in the Hampshire Record Office.

102. Students of the training college, seen here at the outbreak of the First World War. These men were the winners of the dormitory competition, representing 'Arx' as the Ark on their shield bears witness, although an alternative tradition says their bandages bear witness to a bruising game of rugby with St Luke's College, Exeter!

103. Peter Symonds' school *c.*1909 during the headship of the Rev. Telford Varley, M.A., B.Sc. The school stood in seven acres of ground, facing south, and cost £9 2s. 6d. per annum for tuition (including stationery and games) and £35 per year inclusive for boarding.

104. Winchester Modern school was built on the Romsey Road, *c.*1880 at the expense of Lord Northbrook, sometime Viceroy of India. Its successor, Westfields failed by 1897 when Lionel Helbert founded West Downs. The third and final headmaster was Olympic silver medallist Jerry Cornes who officiated from 1954 until 1988. Recession has for the moment prevented development of the site, but the main building which remains empty is now in a dilapidated state. Notable old boys include Oswald Mosley, two sons-in-law of Churchill — Sandys and Soames; the late Nicholas Ridley, Jeremy Morse the Chairman of Lloyds Bank, Peter Scott, Richard Ingrams and David Astor.

105. Exeter House prep school boys *c*.1910, outside the building adjoining the Baptist church on City Road. At that time the house was shared by the Inge family, which included both a doctor and a dentist.

106. Henry White's school outfitters, *c*.1916, moved into 30 High Street, at the western end of the Pentice in 1896. The premises have recently been occupied by Thomas Cook the travel agents, who had formerly been further up the street on the other side of the road.

107. Stanmore Junior school, Class 2 in 1929. The school had just been built, so these children must have been amongst the first to study there.

108. St Swithun's school for girls opened in 1884. It was originally at 17 Southgate Street, but moved to North Walls until 1930. The buildings seen here after being empty for some years were tenanted by the Tax office and the School of Art, and other organisations. The County Library Headquarters has now occupied the premises for some years. This picture was taken from the tennis courts, soon afterwards to be covered by the bulk of the Odeon Cinema, which is now replaced by a sheltered housing scheme.

109. Girls from St Swithun's (or possibly art school students), seen here working in a drawing class in this pre-war photograph.

110. St Swithun's transferred to a new site on Alresford Road, shown here. The architects were Mitchell and Bridgewater of London. The girls moved in on 30 October 1930, but the official opening was not for another two years. Amongst its greatest supporters in the transitional stage was Bishop Theodore Woods, who sadly died just before the official opening. In a recent computation of public examination results in the autumn of 1992, the girls were reckoned to have achieved a higher place in a league table of results than the boys at Winchester College.

Working Day

Archaeology has revealed much about the world of work in ancient and medieval Winchester as the publication of *Object and Economy* (1990), by Martin Biddle, shows. The medieval industry of clothmaking was already withdrawing from the city in the 15th century. Since then the city has developed more as a market and service centre for the locality although with some industry. This change is reflected in the pictures selected in this section.

The spaces within the city enabled the mixed manufacturing and residential character of the medieval town to be recreated in the modern period. The Winchester City Foundry, which closed in the early years of this century, was at Middle Brook Street and made amongst other things, parts for the G.W.R. Some streets, like St Swithun's Street, have until recently retained elements of that mixed economy: church, residential property, building trades, auto-electrical workshop — all on one side of the street. Notwithstanding this mix the street boasted in the 19th century a bakery and a brewery, together with a number of other activities, such as straw hat making. Elsewhere, residential areas have become more firmly defined, for example, round the corner in Canon Street (illustration 34).

The main employer in the city today is the County Council, and its city counterpart, with such industrial activity as still exists largely confined to the Winnall Industrial Estate, developed since the 1950s (illustration 30). Work today involves office tasks for many, shop work — but in the centre of town now in chain stores of one kind another, with the family businesses seen here driven to the margins.

111. William Savage's 'Wykeham' studio in St Michael's Road, off Southgate Street. In this studio, Savage worked on a collection of photographs of the city and other views taken between c.1865 and c.1900. A collection of his work and many other photographic collections are in the City Museum.

112. The long-demolished Durngate, in the angle of the walls between the Eastgate and the Northgate, has never been located securely, although some interesting timber-work and sluices were uncovered in recent works near *The Willow Tree Inn*. The Durngate mill, seen here, vanished 25 years ago, except for some machinery south of the bridge. Amongst the millers was William Craze before 1880, about the time this picture, and another of the interior, were taken by Savage. The small bridge in the foreground has recently been supplanted by a splendid new structure, erected by the County Council.

113. Before the First World War, many people in Winchester were employed in the households of wealthy families. This view of a family in the garden of Hyde Vicarage was sent to a friend on a wet August day in 1905 by a member of the household — though not, judging by the poor spelling and lack of punctuation, by a member of the family. The writer expressed the hope of a meeting with a girlfriend from Southsea.

114. Collis's Dairy at 68 Hyde Street, shown on a card posted in July 1907 which declares, 'as you will see by the card we have again been successful at the parade', in this case, a parade of milk floats. Mr. Collis had a farm at Headbourne Worthy which supplied his dairy.

115. The fire at Lion Brewery in mid-August 1908 must have interrupted the working day in Eastgate Street. The building remained a brewery until after the First World War. In 1932 it was a 'stores' and subsequently became the Co-op Bakery which survived until the redevelopment of that area of Eastgate Street into council flats in the 1960s, when the eastern stretch of Friarsgate was created.

116. Minstrels' restaurant at 18 Little Minster Street was previously a piano workshop for Teague and King, and before that Offer's (1894-1926). Here we see (*from left to right*), George Offer, his father John, and his two brothers Ernest and Alfred. Mr. Targete an employee of Offer & Co. is on the right with the firm's handcart.

117. This picture taken *c*.1906-1910 shows Ellen Firth the licensee of *The Post Office Tavern* in Parchment Street. Mrs. Firth, who is seen with a relation and her second husband (*left*), may have had other relations in Leeds where this card was addressed. Such connections were not unusual in Winchester where, as the censuses show, many of the residents came from scattered geographical origins. The large number of licensed premises employed many migrants to the city.

118. Warren's Wykeham Press, *c.*1910. For many years, a substantial amount of Winchester printing was undertaken here, including a magnificent series of trade directories. However, in a desperate rush for metal early in the Second World War, all the type was sent for war supplies, and the press published no more directories for over a decade. The traditional arrangement of upper and lower case can be clearly seen.

119. Hunt & Co., chemists, occupied the corner site of High Street and Little Minster Street for many years. Hunt's disappeared *c.*1980 to be replaced by The Edinburgh Woollen Mill. The interior of the shop was photographed, perhaps in the 1930s, together with the rear workshop where the large pestles and mortars for crushing the powders were located. The business lives on, now in Silver Hill. Apothecaries had traded in this part of the High Street since the 18th century. The wealthy Mr. Earle's house at 105 High Street (now the National Westminster Bank) was built *c.*1750, indicating that this most central part of the city's main commercial area once contained residential property.

120. This picture of Jewry Street was taken *c*.1916, and shows a soldiers' canteen on the left. Across the road in the converted 1805 prison building are A. G. Rider's studio and William Stopher's ironmongery business. Incidentally, William Stopher gave his place of birth in a census as Pimlico, in contrast to Thomas Stopher who wrote of his father being from Saxmundham, Suffolk. William Stopher's shop subsequently became Dibben's, in the same line of business.

Shopping

The medieval St Giles's Fair drew traders from all over Europe. The city markets, closed during the St Giles's Fair on the orders of the bishops, thrived for the rest of the year. The Buttercross in the High Street may indicate the site of its eponymous market; a beast market took place at the north end of Jewry Street, although since October 1936 the enlarged cattle market, closed in July 1989, took place off the Worthy Road, currently a site for the ubiquitous car boot sales on Sundays. The market house and *The Market Inn* at the south end of The Square indicate former market associations. The market house of 1772 survives nearby, now partly empty. In recent years markets were regularly held in the old central car park site, but the development of the Brooks Centre forced the traders to find another site further north, although some (non-vehicular) stalls are allowed in Middle Brook Street (illustration 6).

Certain areas of the city have now become 'residential', whilst the High Street, The Square and indeed all the central commercial area is no longer a mixed commercial and residential area, as the 19th-century censuses tell us they once were.

The commercial areas have changed considerably, with wealthy institutions such as building societies and banks replacing the sweet shops and tobacconists of yesteryear on the prime sites. Public houses, once common in the centre of the High Street, have now been pushed to the margins. Whereas before the Second World War men's clothes shops predominated, now women's clothes shops are to the fore. Where family businesses once proliferated, since the beginning of this century multiple stores have moved in and now dominate the scene. However, even here change is evident as out-of-town grocery shopping has killed off many of the High Street food stores. Preservation has had an effect on the development of shopping in the centre of the city. Ancient medieval buildings converted into cramped shops, such as the Pentice, require high value, low bulk goods. Amalgamations and take-overs, such as those made early this century by Boots, have enabled some large stores to develop in central positions, but chain stores such as Woolworth's (1929) and Marks & Spencer's (1935) had to redevelop to provide themselves with sufficient accommodation. Recent restructuring of the Woolworth group has led to a further redevelopment on their High Street site, which has resulted in a scaling down of premises into smaller units, perhaps in response to the numerous shop units available in the nearby Brooks Centre.

The arrival of the Brooks shopping centre in recent years follows the 'mall' fashion for shopping which became a common feature of the 1980s. However, central Winchester with its high rents, and with space at a premium, required an especially wealthy developer to take on the large Brooks site. Late in the 1980s a developer for the site was found, but the recession of the '90s has left both High Street and Brooks centre with empty shops as a diminishing number of businesses occupied the premises — as the recent photographs in the 'Then and Now' section show.

Undoubtedly the large group multiple stores have suffered in recent years with the disappearance of chains such as Dewhurst's butchers (Vesty), Top Shop on the High Street and Clothkits in the Square. New niche enterprises flourish such as Past Times, the heritage chain and Boot's Opticians. The history of shopping has much of interest to reflect upon.

121. Stopher's extravagant De Lunn buildings at the north end of Jewry Street were what might now be described as a speculative development of the late 19th century. Before the First World War, Walker's the family grocer was at number four. Today, there are no provision shops left in that part of Jewry Street, although Oliver's fish and chip restaurant serves traditional sustenance (and drinks!) to passers-by and the hungry theatre-goers leaving the Theatre Royal across the road. Some of the De Lunn buildings now lie empty.

122 & 123. Gudgeon's at 38 High Street in the late 19th century. Robert Gudgeon arrived in Winchester from Eye in Suffolk *c*.1812 and set up in business here with £40 borrowed from the St John's Charity. When his descendant R. H. Gudgeon died in 1903, the shop and arcade were sold to Boots for £4,150. The chemist demolished Gudgeon's and the arcade, and spent a further £4,000 building the premises which now occupy this site. The arcade ran through to The Square. Boots preserved the properties they acquired adjacent to the Gudgeon's site so that today these premises conceal the skeleton of a late medieval Wealden house.

124. In 1904 Mr. Powell the butcher sent this picture of his shop at 25 Jewry Street to the Caplin family of Southampton as a Christmas card. The meat on view here represents quite a change from the supplies attributed to the two city butchers before 1850 (illustration 48). Powell's display is framed by quarters of beef with sides of beef below and legs of lamb above.

125. Just along the road was George Ward's poultry and fish shop at 47 Jewry Street, seen here in 1905. A fine display indeed, and very much a period piece, for who would hang meat outside their shop in the fume-ridden atmosphere of today even if the health inspectors would allow it!

126. A view of The Square in 1905, with the recently-opened museum to the right. Chalkley's fishing tackle, sports and taxidermist's shop occupied this corner site for over half a century until it disappeared, c.1960. The large fish was passed to a similar business, The Rod Box, which traded for a period in appropriate goldfish-bowl premises in St George's Street, now part of D. & G. Hardware. Chalkley's own premises passed in time to Clothkits, a clothing chain, but they withdrew in recent years to be replaced by Write Up, a card and fancy goods business which, under different management, had traded next door. This has now closed and the corner property's new tenants are reproduction furniture dealers.

127. This picture was taken *c*.1906. Allen's sweetshop was another corner shop business which survived into the early 1960s on the south western corner of the Pentice, and it appears in many pictures of the Buttercross. The site, which was briefly a shoe shop, has been occupied for 25 years by the Anglia Building Society, successors to the Northampton Town and Country Building Society. The property has been extensively renovated to the exclusion of the dormer window and the chimneys (illustration 48). The square-fronted property on the right is currently occupied by the clothes shop Pilot. It is clearly a re-fronted building of some antiquity, and is believed to occupy part of the site of the Norman palace. From 1912-39 it operated as 'The Norman Palace Tea Rooms'.

128. A 1906 view of Kemp's at 153 High Street, which sold a range of postcards to visitors. The business appears to be flourishing but it is only listed in the trade directories in 1908, the premises being in the occupation of B. Pentelow in 1909. Apart from the interest of the posters, the collection of cards in the window contains a number which are readily recognisable to the collector today, for this was the golden age of the postcard (illustration 178). By 1924 the shop had become Churchill's newsagent etc. which it remained until the 1970s after which it became a motor accessory shop. It is now a fabric shop.

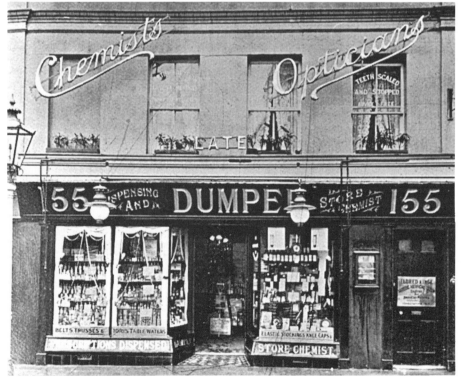

129. Lewis Dumper's 'late' chemist's business (1898-1907), operating under the banner of Eldred and Inge from 1908, was located at 155 High Street in another timber-framed building, re-fronted perhaps in the 18th century. It is still a chemist's business, operated by Pomeroy since the late 1950s. The Dumpers, it is said, at one time occupied no fewer than eight shops in the High Street.

130. David Murray's business flourished for many years from 1902 at 54 High Street, and is unusual in that pictures not only of the exterior, but also of the interior and of Mr. Murray himself have survived. This picture was probably taken before 1921 when the business appears to have merged with that of Mark Hutchings.

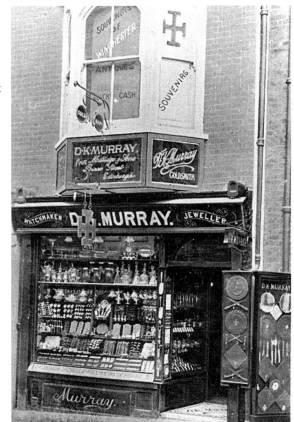

131. Ada Holliday's photography business operated from 1906-20 at 36 Jewry Street (*see* illustrations 120 and 167), near Rider. It was part of a family business; her son ran a branch in Alton. Mrs. Holliday, who described herself as an 'Art Medalist' [sic], has left for posterity a good number of photographs of Winchester. This picture of his rival's establishment was taken by C. E. S. Beloe, *c*.1910.

132. The Maypole Dairy which operated from the site immediately adjacent to the east end of the Pentice,
29 High Street, now part of Richards, is said to have been the first multiple store to appear in Winchester,
established in the early years of the century. This picture, taken c.1915 with the staff outside, is in peaceful
contrast to another from the First World War in which soldiers are seen being hotly pursued by the police after
attacking the Dairy, acting on information that the manager was a pacifist. Upstairs at this time was the
Winchester and Social and Military Club, which before the First World War had been the Liberal Club and
after the War became the Labour Club.

133. Norah Gifford's mother, who sent this missive probably in 1909, found the subject of this picture very interesting as the 'new shop is just finished'. The 'rebuilding' of the International Stores in the Pentice is about to begin. Maybe Miss Gifford was a relation of Gifford the seed and corn merchant who operated nearby from a High Street premises (illustration 69) across the road. Gifford's premises, still vividly recalled in the town by those who bought pet food, amongst other things, was there for many years. It survived various bouts of rebuilding in 1929 and 1989-90 and its chapel-style window can still be seen next to Woolworth's.

134. This excellent display in the World's Stores just before the Second World War includes some familiar brands. From at least 1912 World's Stores was at 137 High Street.

135. Millet's, seen here in 1938, occupied the corner site which linked Jewry Street to St George's Street, with a walkway above. The building was demolished in the interests of road widening, which also brought about the demise of the *George Hotel*.

Worship

The Cathedral Priory and its successor, ruled by the Dean, have dominated the religious life of the city since Norman times. From over 50 churches in the city, the numbers steadily declined until the 19th century, as many churches decayed or were put to other uses. The increase in numbers and size of churches was due to the competition against the established church from both Nonconformists and Catholics, especially after the Emancipation Act of 1829. By this time, there were Catholic and Nonconformist places of worship in the city at 'Milner' chapel in St Peter's Street, and, from 1807, the Independent Congregational chapel in Parchment Street.

In the course of the century many of the old churches were either entirely renovated, as in the case of the ruined church of St Bartholomew's, Hyde, and St Maurice's; or entirely rebuilt, amidst loud protests from those of a historical turn of mind, as with St Thomas's, which was moved to Southgate Street. In addition, entirely new churches were built such as the Nonconformist chapel in Jewry Street and Holy Trinity (both built in 1853) and St Paul's, Weeke (1873), and finally All Saints (1890-98). This century has seen the addition of further churches such as St Peter's (1928), and St Luke's, Stanmore.

136. Amongst the lost treasures of Winchester is the Magdalen Hospital which, like St Cross to the south, stood apart from the city, in this case to the east beside the road to Alresford. Unlike the Almshouse of Noble Poverty, however, Magdalen Hospital, as its name suggests, was associated with lepers, which may have accounted for its isolation. Abandoned by the late 18th century it was demolished because it had become prey to vagrants. This late 18th-century view shows the chapel to the right and the remaining residential building. There are some fine engravings of the interior which then retained a full scheme of painted decoration and fine Romanesque architecture.

137. The Catholic chapel, or Milner Hall, as it is now known, was the Catholic centre in Winchester from the 18th century until a new church was built in 1928. Milner Hall is the most important Gothic revival building in Winchester. It has recently been restored, after experiencing a period of hard times, and much of the original grandeur of this early 19th-century print can once more be enjoyed.

138 & 139. Near the centre of the city, old St Maurice's (illustration 3) was demolished and almost entirely rebuilt by Gover, c.1842. The rural setting, photographed by Savage in 1865, with sheep grazing in the outer close, belies the location of the church. Today, only the tower with its Norman doorway survives, together with fragments of the stone, brick and flint wall which can be seen behind Debenham's.

140. Renewal implies replacement and old St Thomas's was demolished in 1845 to make way for a new church with a steeple, completed in 1857. The new church was, in the opinion of Pevsner, the finest of the new Gothic churches in the city as it incorporated the best features of medieval revival architecture. It was one of the series of 19th-century churches built to serve the needs of the growing population, after centuries of stagnation. It is much altered and has until recently been the Hampshire Record Office.

141. During the 19th century there was much refurbishment of medieval churches in the hope of restoring them to their pre-Reformation splendour. This view of St Cross shows Butterfield's 'Zebraesque' work, which converted the Norman columns into 'barbers' poles', such disdainful terms implying that the restoration was clearly not to the liking of one contemporary. Other contracts by this notable architect included the new hospital (illustration 157) and the complete reconstruction of the chapel tower at Winchester College (illustration 97).

142. The cathedral choir in 1877 when the choir school was at 4 The Close, now the Judges' lodgings. In the back row, second from the right is E. W. Savage, son of the photographer.

St. PETER'S.
CHEESEHILL St.
WINCHESTER.

143. Outside the city walls some of the medieval churches have survived, although this one, St Peter's, Chesil, has become an amateur theatre. This picture, from just before the First World War, shows some timber-framed cottages and *The Brewers Arms*, which ceased trading as a public house *c*.1914. The cottages and the former public house have since been demolished. The more modern house abutting the church is now boarded up, temporarily reprieved from demolition by the recession.

144 & 145. Holy Trinity at North Walls, designed by Woodyer of Guildford, was built in 1853-54, and is reminiscent of the medieval chapels built in the style of reliquaries. It was sumptuously painted inside by Joseph Pippet before 1889. It is now in a shared ministry with St John's. The paintings and much of the fine furniture were destroyed by an 'improving' incumbent in recent years, but in this picture we gain a good impression of the church in the early years of this century.

146. Primitive Methodists in front of the Congregational church which they had borrowed for their quarterly meeting, c.1900. They were not all Winchester people, although the lady in the front with her two sons is Mrs. Prangnell, whose bakery and confectionery business was on the north side of the Broadway (illustrations 77 and 180).

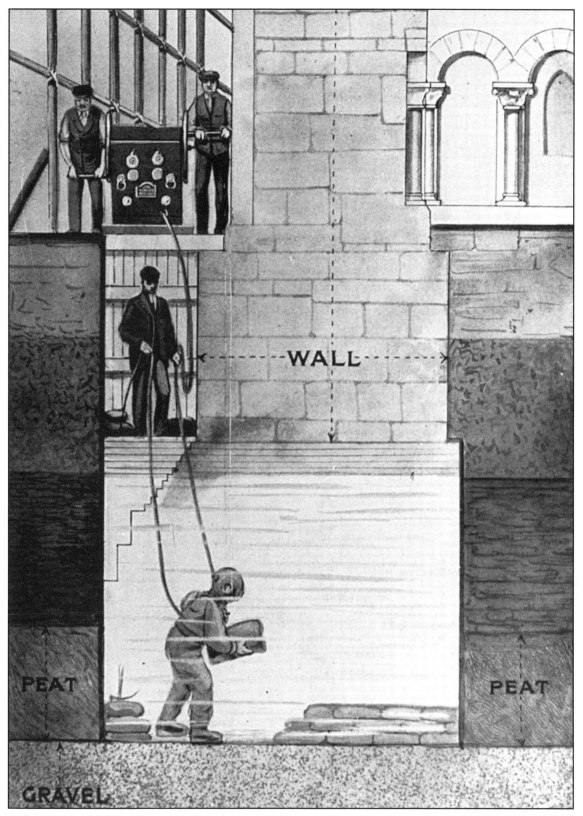

WALL

PEAT

PEAT

GRAVEL

147. The story of William Walker the diver is very well known; without his underpinning work, the cathedral might well have collapsed. This picture gives an impression of the nature of the task he performed between 1907 and 1912.

FOR CATHEDRAL REPAIR FUND

MADE FROM WOOD TAKEN FROM
FOUNDATIONS ETC.
A.D. 1202-1906.

148 & 149. A small industry developed, selling souvenirs made from the wood William Walker excavated. Even today, small wooden objects like those shown in the picture above emerge in the antiques markets of the city. The overseer of the work was Mr. Hill (*below, left*), seen here with the architect J. B. Colson inspecting the huge timber supports which enveloped the east end of the cathedral for some years.

150. Sponsorship is not new. The buttresses on the south side of the cathedral were sponsored by both individuals and groups such as the Mothers' Union who sponsored the two on the right. They may have been selected as they lay closest to 1 The Close, the former home of Mary Sumner, who founded the Union in 1885. Her husband George Sumner, Bishop of Guildford, is commemorated by the buttress on the extreme right. Other buttresses recall former Wykehamists and those who had recently departed, as their incised plaques bear witness.

151. St Swithun's upon Kingsgate is the sole survivor of the city's medieval gate-churches, for prayers before travel. The bell cote is smaller now than it was around the time of the First World War, when this photograph was taken. A further church was sited in St Swithun's Street on the corner opposite Symonds Street in the middle ages, but had disappeared before the Reformation.

152. St Peter's Catholic church, completed in 1928, incorporates a doorway, the only remnant of the Magdalen Hospital (illustration 136). The fine Wesleyan chapel shown on the right is now a film studio, and lies just across St Peter's Street.

153. This 1961 picture of Water Lane, just to the east of the city, shows number 25, known from 1929 onwards as Beeston House, and the adjacent Mission Hall which was run by the Baptists until it was demolished in the early 1960s.

154. The cathedral choir in May 1990 under their current organist and choirmaster, David Hill, who recently took many of this group on a concert tour to Brazil and has embarked upon an ambitious programme of recording.

Health and Welfare

A monument to the plague of the 17th century is still to be seen outside the Westgate, erected where food was left for the beleaguered inhabitants. Low profiles of plague pits can still be made out a mile or so from the city, by the southern slopes of St Catherine's Hill. The plagues which beset the city between 1348 and the 1660s disappeared as suddenly as they had come, but the population did not immediately increase.

Recovery began from 1800, and with the resurgence in population drainage problems, which had been a bone of contention between the monasteries in The Close 700 years earlier, resurfaced. The city within the crowded walls was struck by cholera, and fierce debate arose amongst the citizens as to whether there should be new drains. Fundamentally the disputants fell into two categories: those who had the wealth, that is to say the major institutions, who were against the new drains, and those who would benefit, but lacked the resources to provide. The battle of the 'muckabites' raged to and fro with abusive songs (one with the refrain 'Hey-ho, Stink-O'), but the drains were not built until 1878.

Winchester's damp centre became synonymous with sickness which no doubt encouraged the removal of the hospitals and other amenities to the West Hill. The Training College, formerly at Wolvesey, suffered a serious outbreak of illness. This encouraged Bishop Sumner and his energetic supporters, who included John Keble, to finance a new building on a West Hill site, which opened in 1862.

In recent years many private nursing homes and residences for the elderly have been established in the city alongside the public welfare institutions.

155. The hospital has relocated three times in a quarter of a millennium. This engraving of 1812 shows the Colebrook Street hospital. Some relics from the demolition can now be seen in the City Museum.

156. Beneath the sunny villas of Parchment Street today are the remnants of the inadequate drains of this large hospital, seen here c.1865. Attempts to locate hospitals in the centre of town were bedevilled by problems of drainage; the same problems which had contributed to the decision of the monks of the New Minster to move to Hyde in 1110.

157. Fresh air, a green field, and a hilltop site to cure the drainage problems once and for all, led to the building of the Hampshire County Hospital on the West Hill c.1868, later dubbed 'Royal' by special permission of Queen Victoria. It joined other amenities, which had formerly been situated within the city walls; the West Hill Cemetery (built in 1840), the Diocesan Training College (1862), the gasworks, the prison (1846-49) and the police headquarters (1847). This view of the prison, hospital and surrounding buildings, was taken in August 1921, and shows just how well aerial photography had developed during the First World War.

158. The Westgate, seen here c.1911, was flanked on the north side by *The Plume of Feathers*. Its castellated western part, which had survived less than a century, was demolished in 1938. The drinking fountain in the foreground was erected by Lancelot Littlehales in 1880 in memory of his mother Ann, but was moved in 1935 to Oram's Arbour, to make way for an island for traffic signs. At this time the provision of public water supplies by private donors was common; for example, the horse-trough located in Jewry Street was erected in memory of those animals which died in the Boer War.

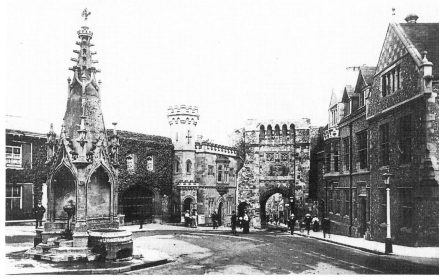

43678 Winchester

159. Amongst the amenities offered in the Lower High Street (seen here before the days of the Alfred statue 1901), were the public baths. Although these have long since disappeared, baths were still available in recent years (at least for ladies), upstairs in the conveniences by St Maurice's tower. Note the appearance of the Art School (*right*) since 1873 (illustration 49)

Wartime and Military Matters

Since the Conqueror's time Winchester has been a military depot. Only in recent years has the castle site been abandoned for the purpose-built Flowerdown barracks. The white elephant of the unfinished royal palace, on the site of part of the medieval castle, went through a variety of uses — as a refuge for French priests at the time of the Revolution, as a prison for enemy captured in the Napoleonic wars — until it settled as a barracks in the 19th century. The palace/barracks was burnt out in 1894 but the building was replaced. The long term future of the site is not certain, but excellent military museums are currently accommodated there. Many houses in the city, for example in the St James's Lane area, were built for military personnel. Army quarters still dominate the area to the south of the West Hill Cemetery.

The cemetery contains 116 war graves and those of eight interned German civilians. Amongst the distinguished heroes laid to rest in the cemetery are Lt. Francis Brown V.C., a hero of the Indian Mutiny in 1857, and Lt. Col. Tongue of the South Wales Borderers. Lt. Col. Tongue took the colours of the regiment, recovered from an African river by Melvill and Coghill during the Zulu wars of 1879, to Queen Victoria at Osborne House in 1880 at the queen's request. Tongue's tomb no longer survives. Also buried at West Hill is Capt. Charles Foss who won his V.C. at Neuve Chapelle in 1916. Neither of the V.C.s died in Winchester: Brown in the Sudan in 1895, and Foss in London in 1953. In a manner reminiscent of those days of Empire, Brown had been born in India and Foss in Japan.

The military value of the city was recognised during the Boer War; trophies such as a howitzer captured by the Rifle Brigade at Ladysmith were brought to the city. The High Street was already adorned by an exceedingly antiquated gun captured from the Russians during the Crimean War half a century earlier. With an important port at Southampton, many foreign soldiers visited the city, and a major international gathering of military attachés met in the city where the War Minister had his H.Q. in 1910.

1914 brought a fragmentation to the different alliances of soldiers who had gathered in the city four years earlier. Many pictures survive of tanks, troops, nurses and all the paraphernalia of war in the city during the First World War. The Second World War again brought the tramp of military boots, not only of the regulars, but also of the Home Guard, to be followed in the 1950s by national servicemen.

160. The old palace barracks *c*.1800 with the medieval castle hall on the right.

161. This picture was taken after the fire of 1894 which gutted the building. The Prince of Wales came to the city to lay the foundation stone of the replacement building which now occupies the site. Its fabric incorporates elements of architectural decoration from the royal palace which are seen here.

162. The First Volunteer Battalion Hampshire Regiment in the High Street, June 1905.

163. The menu at the Hampshire Regiment depot on 5 September 1910. It is not clear why B Company was offered roast beef, followed by rice pudding, while C Company was offered only brown tomato stew and plain pudding.

164. Canadian troops in Jewry Street in 1910. They are proceeding informally along the road to say the least! The Hyde Brewery is just visible in the background.

165. In 1910 the War Minister made the *George Hotel* his H.Q. This picture of the attachés shows the wide range of attenders who assembled for the group photograph in the Winter Garden area of the hotel. In the back row, left to right: Dutch, British, French, Japanese, Norwegian, Austrian, German, British, American, Spanish. Middle row: Serbian, Chinese, Chilean, Russian, Swedish, Italian, British, Japanese, British. Front row: Belgian, Brazilian, Portuguese, Russian, British, Danish, Bolivian, Bulgarian and Turkish.

166. In 1914 Private Lilley sent this card to his sister in Leicester: 'Dear A, Just a line to tell you that I have just enlisted. Am at Winchester & having a fine time. Love from your brother Edgar'. Edgar Lilley, No. 4, Coy K.R.R., no. R 7463. Private Lilley, it seems, survived the war.

167. Soldiers marching down the High Street during the coronation celebrations for George V in 1911. Holliday's picture was taken from the roof of the old Guildhall, now Lloyd's Bank. Note *The Dolphin* and Murray's on the left (pictures 18 and 130).

168. The Judges, who had leased 4 The Close at a low rent as their lodgings on 99-year leases since 1797, gave it up briefly to be used as an auxiliary military hospital run by V.A.D. and St John's ambulance, *c*.1915.

169. Chesil Street with war posters summoning help for the army, and enjoining men to 'Enlist Today', *c*.1916.

170 & 171. Winnall Down camp in verse — a suitable place for 'Kaiser Billy' as it was labelled 'The stockade or prison camp Winnall Down'. It was probably on the site of the old Magdalen leper hospital (illustration 136), although the camp stretched over the Downs to Easton.

WINNAL DOWN CAMP.

THERE'S an isolated, desolated spot I'd like to mention,
Where all you hear is "Stand at Ease," "Slope Arms,"
"Quick March," "Attention."
It's miles away from anywhere, by Gad, it is a rum 'un,
A chap lived there for fifty years and never saw a woman,

There are lots of little huts, all dotted here and there,
For those who have to live inside, I've offered many a prayer
Inside the huts there's RATS as big as any nanny goat,
Last night a soldier saw one trying on his overcoat.

It's sludge up to the eyebrows, you get it in your ears,
But into it you've got to go, without a sign of fear,
And when you've had a bath of sludge, you just set to and
groom.
And get cleaned up for next Parade, or else, it's " Orderly
Room,"

Week in, week out, from morn till night, with full Pack and
a Rifle,
Like Jack and Jill, you climb the hills, of course that's.
just a trifle.
"Slope Arms," "Fix Bayonets," then "Present," they fairly
put you through it,
And as you stagger to your hut, the Sergeant shouts "Jump
to it."

With tunics, boots and puttees off, you quickly get the habit,
You gallop up and down the hills just like a blooming rabbit,
"Heads backward bend," "Arms upward stretch," "Heels
raise," then "Ranks change places,"
And later on they make you put your kneecaps where your
face is.

Now when this war is over and we've captured Kaiser Billy
To shoot him would be merciful and absolutely silly,
Just send him down to WINNAL DOWN there among the
Rats and Clay,
And I'll bet he won't be long before he droops and fades away.

BUT WE RE NOT DOWNHEARTED YET!

172. The *Soldiers Home*, now called *The Welcome*, between the Guildhall and C & H Fabrics, formerly *The City Tavern*. The *Soldiers Home* encouraged soldiers to drink in a temperance atmosphere.

173. Tank 223 in the High Street, *c*.1918. These tanks were awarded to towns which had responded particularly generously in purchasing War Bonds. They were usually Bovington training tanks and were sent by rail to the nearest station, and then trundled the last part of their journey to a pre-arranged site, where, disabled by their crew, they remained as memorials. A postcard sent in 1923 shows the tank penned up in a park in the city, probably Abbey Gardens.

174. An Austin armoured car visiting the city plastered with 'Buy Victory Loan' stickers in a late campaign for sales, on 4 July 1919. These Austins were originally intended for Russia but were witheld after the Revolution and then issued to the 17th (Armoured Car) Battalion, Tank Corps, operating in France, during the summer of 1918. A similarly decorated Austin was photographed in Birmingham during the 'Save for Victory' campaign — perhaps the same machine.

175. The Duchess of York visiting the city in 1939 when she inspected a guard of honour in the High Street.

176. Lord Wavell inspects a guard of honour of the Winchester Home Guard after receiving the freedom of the city, September 1943.

Leisure and Special Events

The city has been host to fairs since the days of the great international St Giles's fair in the middle ages. Fairs and circuses still visit during the summer months. National as well as local events have provided the opportunity for celebrations. This century has witnessed more coronations and Royal visits (illustration 185) than the 19th century when none of the monarchs made an official visit to the city. Queen Victoria frequently visited Osborne House, Isle of Wight, via Southampton which must have brought her through the city. On one such journey in 1897, the year of her Diamond Jubilee, she was welcomed at the railway station.

George V and Queen Mary came to Winchester for the completion of the repair works in the Cathedral in 1912. Edward VIII came as Prince of Wales to visit the city, Stanmore in particular. George VI and Queen Elizabeth came in 1946. The present queen has visited on several occasions, notably in November 1947 on the way to Broadlands, Romsey, after her wedding. As queen she has visited regularly in: 1955 to commemorate the 800th aniversary of the earliest surviving charter, 1959 to open the County Council building named in her honour, in 1967 to review the Royal Green Jackets as Colonel-in-Chief and 1979 when she dispensed the Royal Maundy money.

There is now much more potential for leisure activity than in the past. The old North Walls fields, which boasted little more than a few rowing boats in the 1960s — but what fun they were — now contains the River Park Leisure Centre, which dramatically burnt down in January 1987 and was reopened in 1988. The Leisure Centre also possesses a range of sports pitches to add to the George V fields, Bar End. No doubt for the many commuters, who travel daily to London and elsewhere, the leisure facilities provide a welcome opportunity for relaxation at the weekend.

177. A fair in the Broadway around the turn of the century.

178. Winnall Moor frozen over, *c*.1906. This card can be identified in Kemp's shop window (illustration 128).

179. In 1908 a 'great blizzard' enveloped the city. Beloe the photographer, who lived just off Worthy Road, took this picture near his home. An earlier one in the series shows the faithful postman struggling up to his knees through snow (picture 86).

180. In 1908 the famous gun riot occurred when the mayor decided that the railings should be removed from the Russian gun captured in the Crimean War. The gun had been presented to the city, where it was placed in the Broadway. This picture was taken at the height of the riot in May that year. Joe Dumper who led the riot is seen with his foot on the barrel of the gun. Amongst the acts of violence perpetrated at this time was the depositing of one of the pageant carts from the city pageant in the river at the City Bridge (illustrations 39 and 40). The corner of Prangnell's baker's and confectioner's shop can be seen on the right (illustration 146).

181. The Hampshire Harriers meeting in January 1908 outside *The Eagle Hotel*, 18 (before *c*.1884, 7) City Road on the corner with Andover Road. The reverse of the card, to Miss Westbrook at Corhampton Farm, reveals that the writer — possibly the man on the horse here — had only 'got a little damp ... it was rather a hard ride'.

182. Boys from Colebrook House school swimming at the Bull Drove before the First World War. Bull Drove was the earlier name for Garnier Road and the river baths preserved the name. These baths continued in use until *c*.1960, despite competition from the Lido baths in Worthy Road. The latter closed *c*.1970 and the pool has been filled in.

183. Festive decorations at 12-15 High Street for the coronation of George V in 1911.

184. Coronation decorations in St Cross at the same date, looking south.

185. On completion of the cathedral repair works (illustrations 147-9) the city was visited by George V and Queen Mary on St Swithun's Day, 1912.

186. On the May Bank Holiday weekend in 1913, Sydney Pickles, an Australian, brought his Handley Page monoplane by rail from Penarth to fly at Flowerdown, Littleton. Despite the attentions of the Winchester Motor and Engineering Company, the engine of the plane seized. To become airborne Pickles had to fly in with a further machine from Hendon.

187. Despite poor weather, an exciting air-display took place in the presence of Mr. Handley Page himself and watched by throngs of people.

188. This leafy scene was taken in the 1920s. Until *c.*1960 it was possible to hire boats and row through the North Walls Park. The kiosk, where payment was made and oars stored, still survives, but preparation of pitches for team sports and the creation of the River Park Leisure Centre has led to the development of this once wild area of the city.

189 & 190. The premises of Matthews the coachbuilder extended between Middle and Lower Brook Street. In the first picture it is seen in its heyday, *c*.1904, and, in the second, after the premises had been gutted by fire in 1932.

191. The visit of the Prince of Wales (later Edward VIII) to 72 Cromwell Road, Stanmore, on 7 November 1923. Albert Gearing lived in this house from 1923 until the 1950s. The prince's visit coincided with the completion of the first stage of the Stanmore development, and provided an opportunity to make him a Freeman of the city. He is accompanied by Alderman Dyer, Chairman of the Housing Committee.

192. Proclamation of Edward VIII from the Guildhall in January 1936.

193. The Picture House in the High Street lay between Murray's shop and Jacob and Johnson's *Hampshire Chronicle* building by Hammond's Passage. This photograph was taken in the 1930s just before the picture house closed.

194. The hat fair, now a popular annual event, in the Brooks, May 1991.

Select Bibliography

For picture source references see Illustration Acknowledgments in the preliminary pages.

Atkinson, T., *Elizabethan Winchester*, Faber (1963)

Bailey, C., *Transcripts of the Municipal Archives of Winchester*, Winchester (1856)

Ball, C., *An Historical Account of Winchester with Descriptive Walks*, Winchester (1818)

Carpenter Turner, B., *Winchester*, Phillimore (1992)

Biddle, M., *Object and Economy in Medieval Winchester*, Oxford (1990)

Biddle, M. and Clayre, B., *Winchester Castle and the Great Hall*, H.C.C. (1983)

Crook, J., *A History of the Pilgrims' School*, Phillimore (1991)

Freeman, R., *The Art and Architecture of Owen Browne Carter (1806-1859)*, Hampshire
    Papers, 1 (1991)

Furley, J. S., *The Usages of Winchester*, Clarendon (1927)

Hichens, M., *West Downs*, Pentland Press (1992)

James, T. B., 'The population size of Winchester over 2,000 years: A survey', *Hampshire Field
    Club and Archaeological Society Newsletter*, New Series 9 (1988)

James, T. B. and Doughty, M. W., *King Alfred's College, Winchester: A Pictorial Record*,
    Sutton (1991)

Keene, D. J., *Survey of Medieval Winchester*, OUP (1985)

Kirby, T. F., *Annals of Winchester College*, Winchester (1892)

Milner, J., *History of Survey of the Antiquities of Winchester*, Nutt and Wells (1839)

Pevsner, N. and Lloyd, D., *The Buildings of England: Hampshire and the Isle of Wight*,
    Penguin (1967)

Roberts, E. V., *In and Around Winchester*, Oxley (1977)

Rosen, A. B., 'Economic and Social Aspects of the History of Winchester, 1520-1670', Oxford
    DPhil thesis (1975)

Stevens P. and Dine D., *Winchester: Seen and Remembered*, H.C.C. (1978)

Warren, W. T. (ed.), *Winchester Illustrated*, Winchester (1903)

Hampshire Chronicle (various dates)

Trade Directories of Hampshire and Winchester by Warren, White, Kelly etc. (1784-1973)

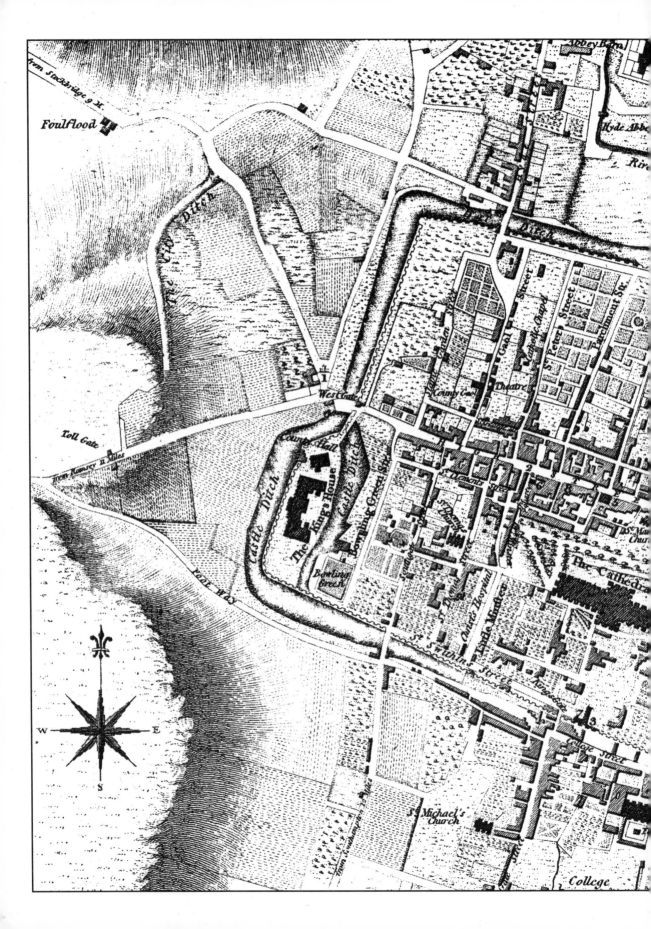